VOYAGE INTO THE PAST

"of Human Asteroids"

by
CARL T. ENDEMANN

A.D. 1373

ALTA NAPA PRESS
Calistoga, California 94515
Publishers
MCMLXXXI

DEDICATION

Two persons close to me, two distinguished authors who consented to become auditors looking over my shoulders, constantly inspiring and sometimes editing:

Professor Edmond Bordeaux Szekely,
last heard of in Cartago, Costa Rica,
and
Professor Georg Theobald Endemann,
last heard of in Kassel, Hessen, Germany.

Strangely, they both seem closer to me now than before they passed on up to Mount Olympus. Much of my communication with them was in Latin — for thousands of years the universal language of scholars and priests.

SIC TRANSIT GLORIA MUNDI? — NUNQUAM! —
MONUMENTUM EXEGI AERE PERENNIUS.
CAROLUS MINOR

INTRODUCTION

What a treat it is to read a book produced by a litterateur such as Carl T. Endemann. His awesome scholarship shines throughout this panoramic presentation as it transports the reader on a journey through the vistas of time.

In *Voyage into the Past,* the author has woven a word tapestry that depicts the peregrinations of a very active soul. Using a delightful blend of prose and poetry, he writes on many levels about his varied experiences.

This volume is a landmark which will serve as a beacon for those intrepid questers who are searching for answers as they attempt to make their way through the esoteric estuaries of enlightenment.

Throughout history there have been unique individuals such as Carl T. Endemann who possess a rare blend of intellect, vision and courage. These people have charted courses through life that endeavor to broaden the horizons of humanity. This to me is a testament to that tradition.

So sail on with the Sage of Alta Napa on a transcendental trip through the regal realm of reincarnation.

Mark Douglas

Table of Contents

For other recall and reincarnation poems, refer to the book, "VOYAGE TO GONDWANA":

Page 48 — Viking in Vinland. 1000 A.D.

Page 49 — When Blue Blook Bleeds. 1703 A.D.

Page 50 — The Ballad of the Cavalier. 1644 A.D.

Pages 70-75 — Kingfisher's Man. 1460 A.D.

Pages 78-83 — Voyage to Gondwana. 1542 A.D.

Pages 84-87 — Jungles of Gondwana. (Cretaceous Period.)

Page 107 — Tiresias. 1500 B.C.

Page 122 — Driftwood. 1180 B.C.

Page 114 — Mythos.

Refer to the book, "FORKS IN THE ROAD":

Page 19 — Roman Road.

Page 41 — Sondershausen Junction. 1910

Page 44 — The Great Revolving Door.

ACKNOWLEDGMENTS

To the many who have helped me in one way or another with this book, I wish to express my appreciation, especially to Sandra Springstun and Judith A. Pressey who did the paintings, and those who helped me researching quotations and other background references, for many months regarding with indulgence my impatience in trying to locate needles in the haystacks of their book stacks:

Clayla Davis, Millie de Jager, June Inghram, Barbara Kaiser; and to Phyllis May Franzmann, who was my editor. Last but not least to Johann Georg Heck for this pictorial inspiration the "Iconographic Encyclopaedia."

Preface

Since time immemorial people have wondered what exactly there is to us besides the physical body with its genes and chromosomes.

Is there an individuation, a monad, a personality?

Or, is there just an emanation of an universal soul, which rises from the cosmic ocean like water in the sunshine and later condenses into particles of mist or snow, or drops of water, and returns after a short "life" — as say a snowflake — to the great world mother ocean, the universal soul or atman, atem, ammon, amen?

"Ignoramus, ignorabimus," said the ancient philosophers: "We do not know and we shall not know."

Since in nature nothing is ever lost, not even the elusive gases, there should be some traces of the unknown factors, even if only on a transcendental level.

We have considerable evidence that there are intangible factors besides the genetical ones, which appear to be transferred or recycled through several lives.

In his book, THE INDEFINITE BOUNDARY, the author G.L. Playfair reports an interesting working hyopthesis worked out by H.G. Andrade of the Brazilian Institute of Parapsychology. He postulates a Biological Organizing Model (for short: BOM) as a metaphysical counterpart to the physical genes. Linked to the latter, their polarities combine to a magnetic field resulting in the construction, both physical and mental, of a human being.

The object of my book is to study the modes of recycling the physical and metaphysical entities, to incite interest in reincarnation and stimulate further research.

One may wonder what there can be left to be said on the subject which has been the theme for a thousand books — on Reincarnation, Reembodiment, Rebirth, Transmigration, Metamorphosis, Metangismos, Metempsychosis, Metensomatosis, Palingenesis — they are all shadows dancing around the same elusive reality: LIFE.

Much of what has been written in the past is accounts of individual cases, many obtained through regression, numerous others demonstrating through scientifically supervised facts, that reincarnation does take place. These individual accounts, being documented, perhaps prove to the satisfaction of sceptic contemporaries what they have not been willing to accept from the leading minds of all times.

However, the facts underlying the shadow-play of life that we observe, like Plato's famous prisoners from their cave, are still unknown to us.

Hans Holzer, in his book, "Born Again," points out the vast scope that the influence of reincarnation would have on our personal as well as public lives if universally accepted in the Western World. This has probably never been better expressed than by Mr. Holzer, so I obtained his permission to quote him:

"Reincarnation gives man the power of free will and of decision making, which orthodox religions have deprived him of.

"Reincarnation, if generally accepted as factual, would, of course, greatly influence our personal conduct.

"I am referring especially to the conduct in times of war, under conditions of violence, or whenever there is a possibility of taking another person's life. Whenever a man or a woman is faced with the commission of a crime, or of an evil deed (I mean evil in terms of contemporary morality?, there is the possibility of "accumulating karma," that is to say, of mortgaging one's future lifetime in a negative sense. Now, if reincarnation is subject to a universal law of retribution and justice, then an evil deed committed in one lifetime may very well have dire consequences in the next one. The knowledge of this might influence people toward a better life, toward a more moral existence. It may prevent crimes of violence, perhaps even war. This may only be wishful thinking on my part, but it stands to reason that a universal and scientifically accepted conviction that reincarnation is factual would have deep and long lasting consequences in our entire way of life. The common attitude toward death, for instance, would undergo rapid and profound changes, for if there is more than one lifetime to live, surely one could not fear death as the inevitable end. Surely one might even welcome it at times if the existence one suffers could be exchanged for a better one within a short time. The hopelessly ill might very well welcome the continuing life cycle."

CRIME UNDER THE RAJ

For over 2500 years the teaching of Gautama, the founder of Buddism, have proven to have a benign influence on the lives of the people of the sub-continent of India, with the profound belief in karma and reincarnation leading logically to the practice of non-violence.

A striking illustration of how the belief in reincarnation has specifically influenced the general population is shown in the record of the British census of India in 1881, which showed the ratio of those criminally convicted among different groups. The startling revelation is as follows:

1 European out of 274,
1 Eurasian out of 509,
1 native Christian out of 799,
1 Hindu out of 1361,
1 Buddhist out of 3787.

These figures were reprinted in "Tablet," leading Catholic publication in Britain, with this comment:

"The last item is a magnificent tribute to the exalted purity of Buddhism. It appears from these figures that while we effect a very marked moral deterioration in the natives by converting them to our creed, their natural standard of morality is so high that however much we Christianize them, we cannot succeed in making them altogether as bad as ourselves."

The Indian converts had, of course, given up their belief in reincarnation and karma in exchange for the church doctrine of "forgiveness of sins." It should be noted that the teachings of Buddha have also considerably influenced the Hindus, particularly the Brahmans.

Now, a hundred years later, the figures would not be as good, since other faiths (including particularly the new faiths of Marxism, and Christianity) have gained more ground, and violence has increased considerably as a consequence. However, the above figures give us a strong and compelling incentive to spread the idea of Reincarnation.

Unfortunately, by this time Buddhism has almost disappeared from India, and is found mainly East of India now.

Why was there such a difference?

Because INDULGENCES — "forgiveness of sins," and GRACE against cash payments are in exact opposition to THE LAW of CAUSE AND EFFECT. Supposedly the Reformation abolished such practices, but they became prevalent again soon in most if not all religions. The temptation of insuring themselves not only a steady income but also tremendous power over their flock was too irresistible. When combined with the exchange of Theological Insurance for the government against physical protection plus guaranteed salaries from the prices, it was an ideal DEAL.

There is ONE LAW for all, no favoritism on the part of the deity. Therefore, "forgiveness of sins" violates all principles of universal justice and integrity.

NEVER TOO LATE

"Grace" offered by the clergy as an escape from the consequences of criminal acts is simply an illusion and causes innumerable cases of recidivism.

They are selling something they cannot deliver.

Knowledge of reincarnation freed the minds of slaves in Greece, and the spirits of Hindus from the hopelessness of the Indian caste system.

I believe, therefore, that spreading the knowledge of reincarnation would be very helpful in civilizing humanity as a whole.

Many a friend has told me: "I have learned so much lately, too bad it was too late to benefit me."

Maybe such knowledge would have helped in the past, but it is never too late to start applying it now, and especially as it will apply to future lives as well.

Part I
Unexplored Territories

THE GREAT REVOLVING DOOR

UBI SUNT
QUI ANTE NOS FUERUNT?*
Who knows
Just what
Went on before -
Behind the ever-turning door?

The door we enter
When we leave,
And out of which
We came to stay.
As one comes in,
One goes away.

We enter the
Revolving door,
But cannot see
Who went before,
Nor who will follow
In our steps,

Nor see where we
Are next to go;
Not until once more
As before …
We passed through the
Revolving door.

Old Latin saying: "Where are those who come before us?"

Chapter I
Footprints In Time

What is this book about?

Tracking our own elusive footprints!

Years ago, I began to notice some apparent patterns of synchronization in the way certain persons would encounter certain others at definite intervals, or the same groups of persons might be associated in different incarnations. Or, one or more persons would pass certain physical landmarks on this globe, either meeting or not meeting, in accordance with some definite and inter-related rhythm. Were they moving in some sort of pattern of orbits? If so, what made this inter-dimensional "world"-go-round? Was it chance? Here was an intriguing mystery.

Anatole France says: "Chance is a pseudonym God uses when he does not want to sign his own name."

I could find but little information in astrological literature, or in books on reincarnation, and just a few hints in other metaphysical books, or ever in pure fiction - so in order to even scratch the surface of this subject I decided I would have to do my own research, gathering information where I could find it, and perhaps getting contributions from others interested in the subject. For three-quarters of humanity, reincarnation has never ceased to be a simple matter-of-course, but by now also many great minds of the Western World have already recognized the reality of rebirth.

We are simply following in their footsteps.

On the following pages are names of outstanding persons whose works bear witness to their belief in reincarnation.

Louisa M. Alcott	Emily Dickenson
Reverend William Alger	G. Lowes Dickinson
Apolonius of Tyana	Isaac Disraeli
Aristotle	F.M. Dostoevsky
Saint Francis of Assisi	Arthur Conan Doyle
Sir Francis Bacon	John Dryden
Honore de Balzac	Thomas Edison
William Blake	Albert Einstein
Napoleon Bonaparte	T.S. Eliot
Saint Bonaventura	Ralph Waldo Emerson
Robert Browning	Empedocles
Giordano Bruno	Johannes Scotus Erigena
Pearl S. Buck	J.G. Fichte
Sir Edward Bulwer Lytton	Gustave Flaubert
Thomas Campanella	Henry Ford
Thomas Carlyle	Benjamin Franklin
Edgar Cayce	Frederick the Great
Winston Churchill	Robert Frost
Cicero	Paul Gauguin
Samuel T. Coleridge	David Lloyd George
Salvador Dali	Mahatma (Mohandas K.) Ghandi
Charles Dickens	Kahil Gibran

J.W. von Goethe
Robert Graves
Saint Gregory of Nyssa
Rider Haggard
Manly P. Hall
Lafcadio Hearn
G.W.F. Hegel
Max Heindel
Heinrich Heine
Heraclitus
J.G. Herder
Hermann Hesse
Oliver Wendell Holmes
Harry Houdini
Victor Hugo
David Hume
Thomas Huxley
Henrik Ibsen
Dean Inge
William James
Prophet Jeremiah
James Joyce
Emperor Julian
Carl G. Jung
Immanuel Kant
S. Kierkegaard
Rudyard Kipling
D.H. Lawrence
G.W. von Leibniz
G.E. Lessing
H. Spencer Lewis
Charles A. Lindbergh
Sir Oliver Lodge
Jack London
Henry Wadsworth Longefellow
Maurice Maeterlinck
Norman Mailer
Manes
Christopher Marlowe
John Masefield
Somerset Maugham
John Ellis McTaggart
Herman Melville
Cardinal Mercier
Conrad Ferdinand Meyer
Henry Miller
John Milton
Piet Mondrian
Dr. Axel Munthe
Henry More

Lecomte du Nouy
Friedrich Nietzsche
Eugene O'Neil
Ovid
Paracelsus
Archbishop Passavalli
Plato
Plotinus
Plutarch
Edgar Allen Poe
Porphyry
Poseidonios
Proclus
Pythagoras
Ernest Renan
Charles Renouvier
R.M. Rilke
Romain Rolland
J.D. Salinger
Friedrich Schiller
Friedrich von Schlegel
Albert Schweitzer
Arthur Schopenhauer
Sir Walter Scott
W.B. Seabrook
William Shakespeare
George Bernard Shaw
Percy Bysshe Shelley
Jean Sibelius
King Solomon
Alexander Solzhenitzyn
Herbert Spencer
Edmund Spenser
Baruch Spinoza
Rudolf Steiner
August Strindberg
Rabindranath Tagore
Taliesin
Alfred, Lord Tennyson
Ernest Seton Thompson
Henry David Thoreau
Leo Tolstoy
Mark Twain
Dr. Edward B. Tylor
Virgil
Voltaire
Richard Wagner
Walt Whitman
William Wordsworth
William Butler Yeats

Reincarnation has been a part of Egyptian, Greek and Asian philosophies for many thousands of years - all the way back to their beginnings. Some of the best known exponents of reincarnation include:

Plato, considered probably the greatest of all philosophers, who lived and taught in Athens between 427 and 347 B.C. He was a student of Socrates, 469-399 B.C., the great teacher in Athens.

Pythagoras, Greek philosopher and mathematician, musician and astronomer, born in Samos, who taught in southern Italy from 530 B.C. on.

Empedokles, Green philosopher in Akragas, Sicily, 5th century B.C., the same time as Plato was in Athens.

Later, Plotinus, in the 3rd century A.D., a Greek philosopher, born in Egypt and active in Rome. He is the father of Neo-Platonism.

Having read what others said on this theme and everything else I could find on the subject, I wanted confirmation of all these theories.

So I started by checking some of my own memories, mostly obtained by spontaneous recall, but at least partly confirmed by actual visits to different places - Palermo, Agrigento, Como, Gent, Brugge, Paris - trips I undertook for the principal reason of checking up on my possibly too vivid imagination.

The results condensed into a number of poems and essays, and a few letters describing my experiences. They are interspersed with notes, letters and poems I had written before my intense studies began.

They include reincarnation experiences of some friends of mine, and also a number of names, places and symbols, the complete meaning of which still escapes me. They ring some bells though, like distant temple bells.

It may happen that a striking personal incident will make us aware and fully conscious of the existence of the cycles of reincarnation. Such experience came to me and is described in Chapter IV.

Different writers on reincarnation report that some young children, in the first 7 years of their lives, may experience some remembrance of their previous lives, a very few even remembering their previous names. Most frequently, in the Western World, they are discouraged by their parents and peers, and tend to lose the faculty, so most of these cases come from Eastern cultures.

The great American philosopher, George Santayana, has well analyzed the strange situation when he said:

"Those who cannot remember the past are condemned to repeat it."

Perhaps a more acceptable statement would be: Those who do not learn their lessons in one incarnation are assigned them again in the following lives.

The basic law behind this is the Law of Karma: "As ye sow, so shall ye also reap."

In Buddhism and Hinduism, karma is the doctrine of responsibility for all one's actions in all incarnations, that explains and justifies good and evil fortunes.

I quote from "The Secret Doctrine of the Rosicrucians" by "Magus Incognito," written in 1918:

"The Rosicrucians teach that the human soul is on the path of progress, learning the lessons of life and experience, life after life, and storing away the essence of these impressions which go to form the basis of the "character" of the individual when he is reborn. The rebirth, or the conditions thereof, are not forced upon the individual soul, but on the contrary the individual soul is attracted toward rebirth by reason of the presence of certain desires in its character - or rather by reason of the essence of its desires. It is reborn into certain environments solely because it has within itself certain unsatisfied desires which could be satisfied only in just those environments. The operation of the Law of Attraction is justly regular here, as in the attraction of the atoms of matter.

"Each soul contains within itself the attracting force of certain sets of desires, and this force attracts to the soul certain conditions and experiences and also attracts such experiences and conditions to the soul. There is no element of punishment, or of injustice, in the operation of this law, for it gives to each soul just what the soul requires to meet its indwelling unsatisfied desires, or also the conditions and experiences which will serve to burn out of the soul certain desires which are holding it back in its progress, the destruction of which will make possible future advancement.

"Many object to the doctrine of Rebirth on the ground that the experiences of each life, not being remembered, must be useless and without value. This is an erroneous view of the subject, for such experiences are not lost to us at all, but really form part of the material of which our minds are composed. They exist in essence in the form of feelings, characteristics, inclinations, likes and dislikes, affinities, attractions, repulsions, etc., and are in this form just as much in evidence in our lives as are the experiences of yesterday which are well remembered.

"All men and women are what they are by reason of what they have gone through, have lived out and outlived. And though these happenings, scenes, circumstances, occurrences, experiences, have faded from the memory, their effects are indelibly imprinted upon the fabric of the character, and the individual of today is different from what he would have been had the happenings or experience not entered his life.

"You have not the memory of the experiences, but you have the fruit in the shape of characteristics, tastes, inclinations, etc. You have a tendency toward certain things, and a distaste for others. Certain things attract you while other things repel you.

"All this is in accordance with the Law of Attraction which has caused you to attract that toward you for which you have an affinity, and which also causes others to be attracted to you. In the same way, and from the same cause, are the many reunions in this life of persons who have been related to each other in previous lives. The old loves, the old hates, work out in the new lives. We are bound to those whom we have loved, and also to those whom we have injured. The story must be worked out to the last chapter, although an increasing knowledge of the "why and wherefore" of such things may relieve one of many entangling attachments and relationships of this kind."

But we have to give them time.

The beauty of the theory of Karma is that it provides the "Hope of the World" as we strive to sow only the good and reap only the good, or as Hans Holzer so beautifully puts it, "Influence people toward a better life."

Chapter II
Coincidences and Parallel People

I have collected the material for this book through personal experiences, meditation, and by double-checking material offered spontaneously by others. This I will discuss in more detail later on.

As we are going about the little chores in our daily business, we are moving around in certain small orbits which in turn are contained within the scope of larger orbits. See pages 12 to 15 for some diagrams depicting some small orbits that we unconsciously follow.

We travel first to Kindergarten, then to Grammar School, to Stores, to Church, to High School, later to College and to Clubs. We may travel to other cities, other states or on to other countries. A few even have ventured into outer space. Yet we still keep on track in some of the habits or original small orbits, just as satellites and planets on their orbits within orbits of solar systems.

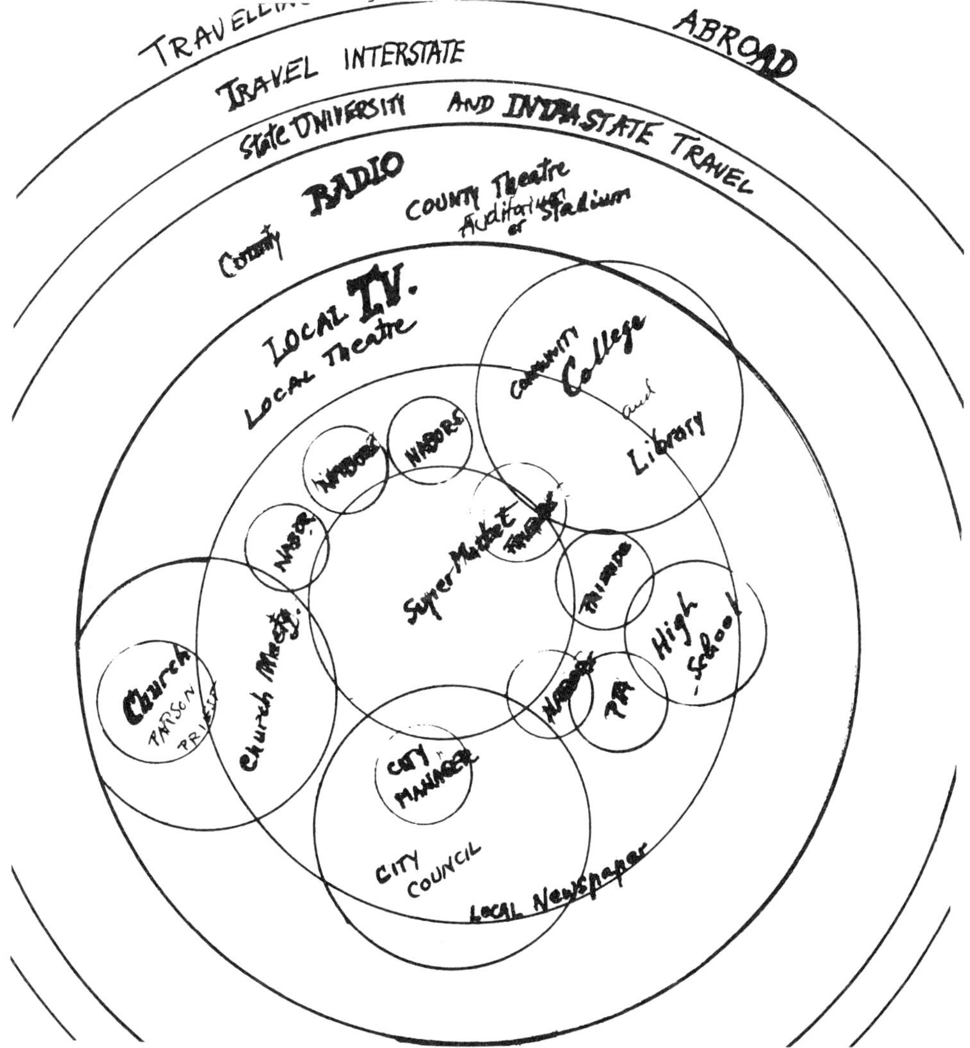

After transition, we continue to move along certain tracks or orbits, which we predetermine to a considerable extent by the pattern of our current life.

Thinking habits, established in us from childhood through family, school and environmental influences, all have created habits of thinking along definite mental tracks which persist and prevent us from considering the reasons which may exist behind the synchronization of events in various people's lives. Many have observed their mental blocks without becoming conscious of their importance, or, even less, their causes.

Often, we encounter other people, and even groups of people, who have travelled over similar tracks and some times so much like our own that we call them "parallel people." At the end of this chapter a good example of parallel people can be found in "Jim Marberry's Story."

It is striking to observe the "coincidental" repeated meetings of people which sometimes occur in a lifetime, and sometimes over several lifetimes. I have an example to offer:

In April 1930 I was watching the passing of the GRAF ZEPPELIN over the city of Brooklyn from the roof-garden of the apartment building where I was living. I became acquainted with another tenant who was watching the passing and we became friends. This was to be the start of a whole chain of events in my life. He introduced me to 4 others, all young lawyers successfully established in their practices in New York. 14 years later I was to meet them all in California, where they had made their homes, all living within a few miles of each other.

If we start observing people in groups, gathering together at different periods of their lives, we find they will be attracted by similar interests and situations. It seems that similar rules apply to groups of people in subsequent incarnations. (Examples later.)

These groups, these migratory birds, or (by way of a cliche) "birds of a feather," seem to fly like migratory birds - or to use another illustration like Asteroids, also called Planetoids - or Comets, Shooting Stars that spin in almost parallel orbits, or at least related orbits.

We travel in circles or ellipsoids, within orbits, in groups. We often meet the same people here and even abroad. Which American tourist has not met abroad people he knew at home?

In our everyday life we revolve around physical centers, fulcra, the existence of which we are not conscious of, but which are nevertheless quite tangible.

We are kept in orbits by magnetic forces that we don't see but which attract or repel us. We move on regular impersonal tracks - to kindergarten, through markets, to houses of friends and family, to schools, to college. Somewhere along the line we become conscious of the fact that we are being pulled out of orbit by personal factors such as class mates, by interest in professions and by more permanent work. We may get drawn into the magnetic fields of sports and hobby groups, religious or philsophical or political associations. Now we are more apt to find more permanent mates and careers.

Gradually we seem to evolve from predominantly physical realms to higher levels of consciousness. We are gradually becoming able to steer our little spaceships within the physical, mental and spiritual limitations that have been given to us.

As we are attracted or repelled by the magnetic fields of forces, some of them may offset or enhance others. Our orbits become adjusted, balanced and steadied on tracks which are the results of external forces and counterforces and our own qualities and limitations of our genetic chromosome combinations.

As below, so above. Similar forces seem to influence our B.O.M.s as they are circulating in and above the Cosmic Ocean. They are attracted and repelled by larger groups now: professions, nationalities, races, family traditions, languages, geographical features, climatological conditions.

Similarly, perhaps planetary ambiences bear on us on mental and spiritual levels.

At some point we are led transcendentally to circulate symbolically amongst planets and galaxies, and we move like comets, shooting stars in different families of showers, and later a bit more steady like asteroids.

I have tried to diagram the undiagrammable on the following sketches.

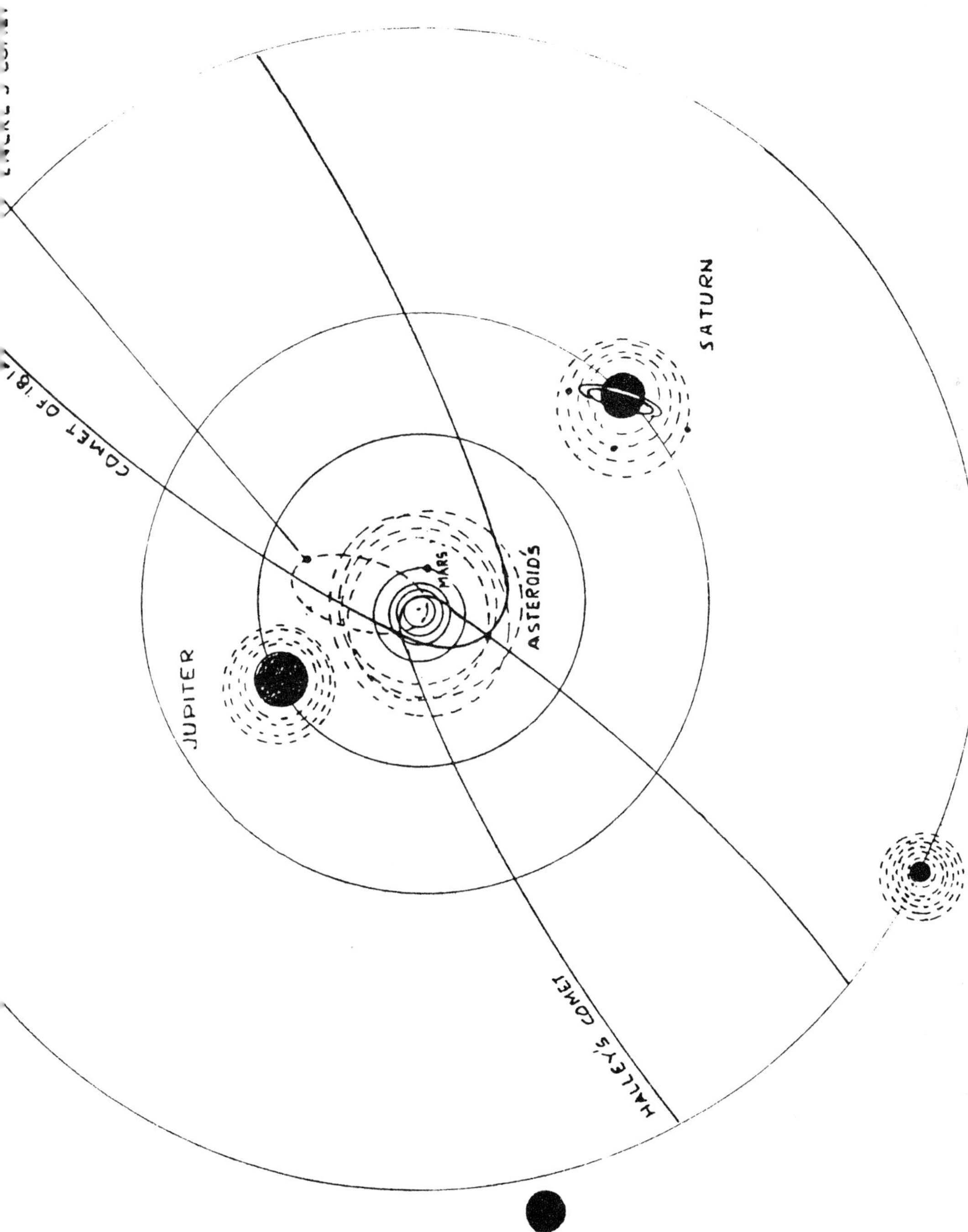

Here Is Another Dramatic Example of Parallel Orbits

Adolf Hitler and Josef Stalin lived just a few blocks apart when they stayed in Vienna in the early 1900s, it was revealed yesterday.

The fact that the two leaders of Nazi Germany and Soviet Union during World War II had been near-neighbors years before was revealed when Vienna police presented the mayor with registration forms of 300 famous or notorious residents.

Until they left Vienna about two yers before World War I, Hitler and Stalin were separated only by railroad tracks and a few apartment blocks in the southeastern suburbs.

Stalin's registration form, filled out in his original name of Josif Djugashvili, gave his occupation as valet for a man called Petrov.

Reuter
London

Figure 2 illustrates how, while following our daily physical routine in 3-dimensional space (as outlined in Figure 1) we simultaneously become subconsciously involved in transmagnetic 4th and 5th dimensional forces. These forces may be emitted by individuals, groups (organizations, clubs, fraternities, cults) which cast magnetic circles. The large circles D and C represent countries, movements or denominations or ideologies, but like oil and water do not mix unless emulsified, under great pressure.

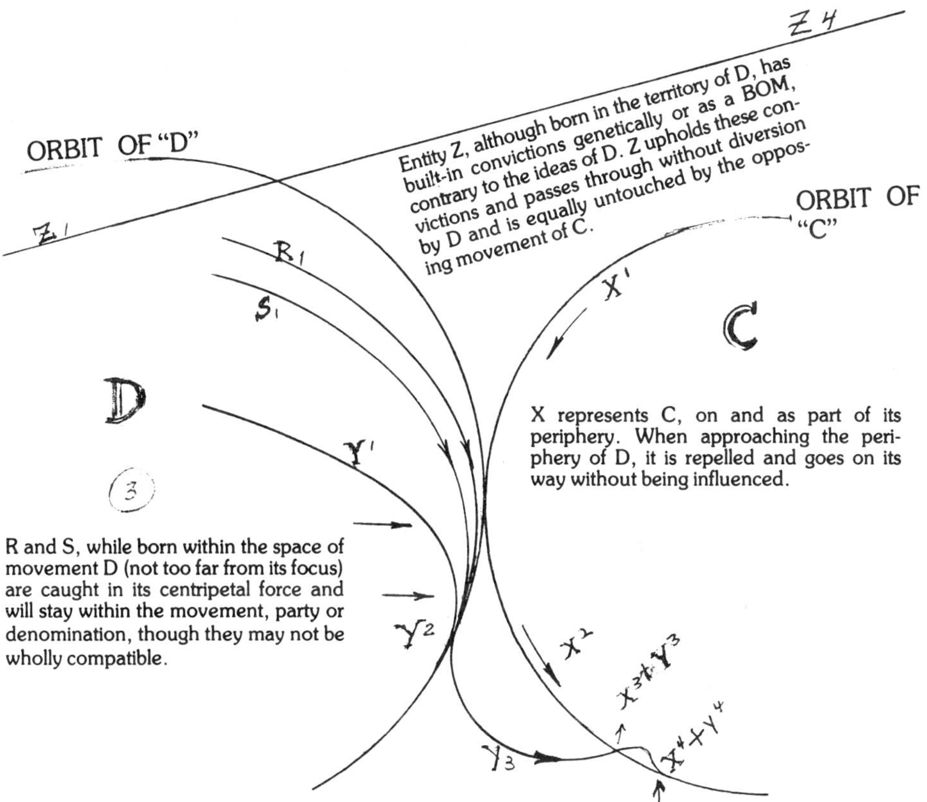

Y, born within the physical/mental confines of D, has met the periphery of D at too sharp an angle of dissent, and escaped when strong forces start to exercise their magnetism. (S)He passes cultural shock, but (S)He meets X, a native of C, an attractive companion and then appears to be harmoniously absorbed into the realm of C. Given Y's independent character, it may be doubtful whether they will end up together, shall we say in Paris, Greece, or separated?

Figure 3. As the weaver intertwines the threads of Warp and Woof to make the fabric, so do impacts of different families on each other intermingle, influencing the fabric of their lives, primarily in a physical way, but also secondarily the thinking and feeling.

TRANSCENDENTALLY, "Deus ex Machina" (as the Antique termed it, or Fate as we call it today) seems to interfere with the (straight?) directions of our lives. We term it the "GREAT WEAVER'S SHUTTLE." Sometimes it leads to permanent entanglements. When invastion of thoughts or of physical people hits our life lines (as a person or a group, or even as a people) AT A RIGHT ANGLE, destruction may result. If the lines meet at more oblique angles, a mixture of ideas, or of religions, or even races, may occur.

Have you observed such interference in YOUR life?

Entity C singly meets all members of Family A at different angles, some more harmoniously, some less, resulting in some degree of relations. D meets the oldest member of Family A (at right angle) (conflict) (mother-in-law?) D meets second member of Family A on a temporarily parallel course, which may result in a permanent bond, such as marriage or partnership.

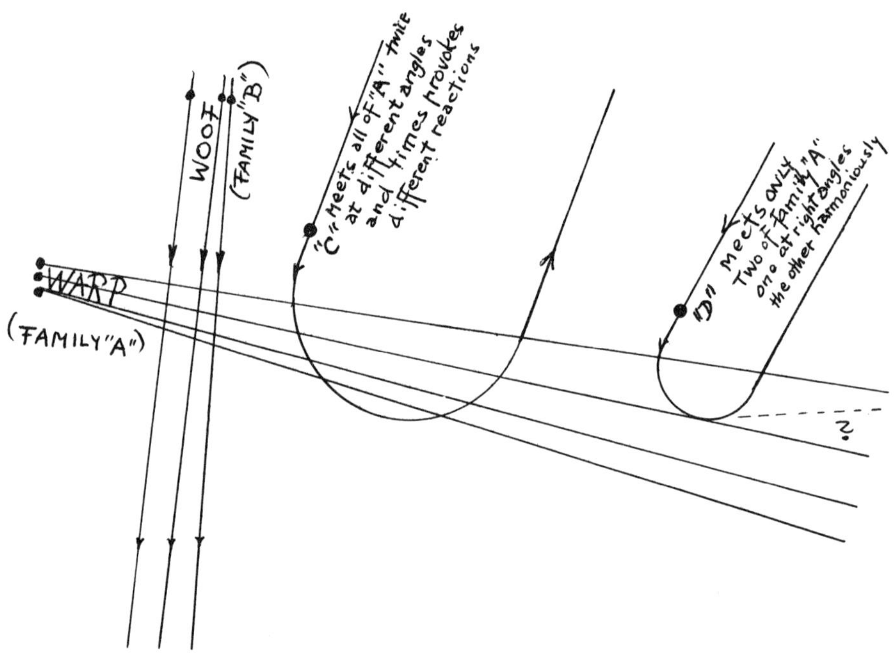

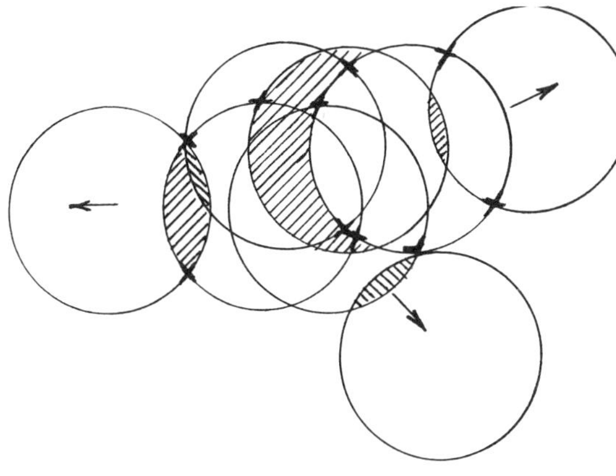

Figure 4. We have different fields of interest to start with, and the aim to move in different directions. In this constantly moving configuration we develop constantly changing common fields of interest with other people (shaded in diagram) and points of sharp conflict (x).

Figure 5. Student A, self-educated, vision not influenced by attending regular classes. B and D go through regular class program and their thinking will be deflected to different degrees, ending up in completely different directions from what their original environment and parental influences started them out with.

Student C takes regular school program, but keeps original attitude and ends up in almost the direction in which (S) he started out with. Many have to conform to demands of jobs, such as a teacher in orbits fixed by the educational system.

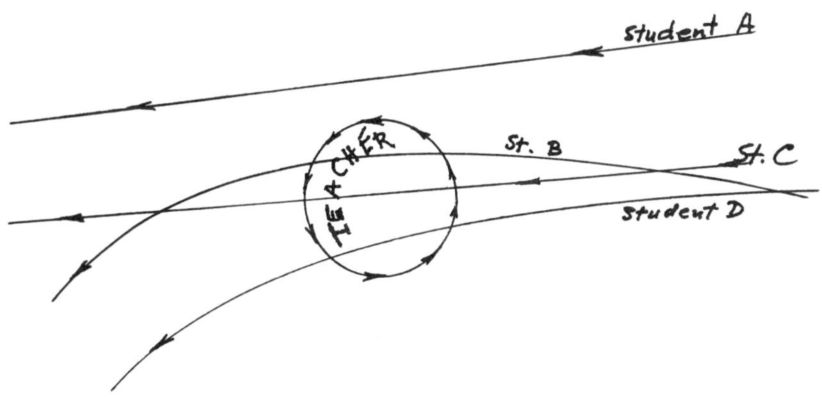

Figure 6. Our fields of interest and activities change slowly but steadily throughout life. We carry forward certain interests and branch out into others. On the average, every 7 years we move into new territories of the mind, parallel to our well known physical transformation and rebuilding of our cells over 7 year periods.

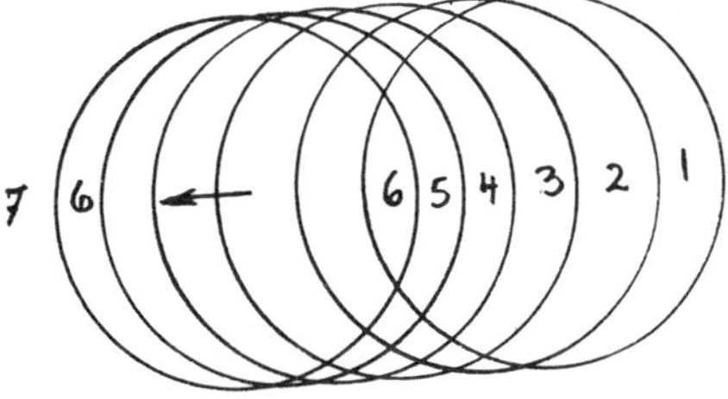

After my dramatic initiation into reincarnation, in the Hotel Cambon in Paris*in the winter of 1932-33, I felt the necessity of checking up on this entire subject. Sceptically, I wanted to know more about it before accepting it. Before I realized it, I found myself enmeshed in an extraordinary chain of coincidences or synchronizations.

On home leave to the U.S. in 1935, I travelled to the West Coast and ended up spending my vacation with friends, at Silver Lake in the high Sierras. With them was a lady from San Jose, California where the headquarters for the Rosicrucian Order A.M.O.R.C. are located. I had heard the Rosicrucian Order taught reincarnation and I was researching this subject. Had she heard about them? Yes, indeed, everybody in San Jose knew about them, and her husband, a lawyer, had handled a law-suit against them! She suggested I see him to learn more.

On the "Cascade" train from Seattle to San Francisco I met a young lady who told me the Rosicrucians were holding a convention in San Jose. All roads seemed to lead me to San Jose!

So I travelled to San Jose and sought out this lawyer. He said he had found nothing wrong with the Rosicrucian Order, that his client had been in the wrong. This was encouraging, and I decided to visit the headquarters myself. I arrived there in the middle of their annual convention. I was very favorably impressed by the well kept grounds of Rosicrucian Park, and the clean-cut, friendly people. Dr. H. Spencer Lewis head of the organization, was extremely busy at this time but nevertheless received me. When I told him I came from Paris, he gave me the name of their representative in that city.

While there, I purchased a book, "Mansions of the Soul," written by him, dealing with the subject of reincarnation, which I read on the steamer on my trip home to France. The book augmented my interest in joining the Order.

In Paris, I called on the representative, Mlle. Jeanne Guesdon, and learned that the organization there was the European "Rose-Croix Universitaire," and was introduced to some students. Being so well received I decided to join the Paris Chapter of the Universitaire in the winter of 1935. I found the teachings were given out very slowly, as the students progressed, which was the way in all metaphysical schools, and wisely so. This became very understandable later when in 1940 the situation turned out to be very dangerous for all philosophical and metaphysical groups on the Continent.

Soon, also, I joined by correspondence the Rosicrucian Order of the U.S., AMORC, as they seemed to be more free to give out important teachings, than the European organizations which were still working under the shadow of the Middle Ages. Their fears, incidentally, soon proved to be more real than anybody had dreamed, but the secret orders had realized it all along. By this time, 1940, I had gained the confidence of the European Rosicrucians, especially the French and Belgian groups who had at first been on their guard, understandably, against an American citizen of German birth and soon to be one of the managers of a French company. I participated in their secret meetings throughout the war. We burnt all incriminating papers, and with particular regret our simple but beautiful white woollen robes in which we were clad when our convocations were held. You will understand why from the original newspaper story which is reprinted herewith.

This certainly was a convincing demonstration that philosophical credos and convictions transcend all political, national or racial limitations which humans are used to imposing upon themselves. Also, it was a practical illustration why there had been so many centuries of delays in spreading the metaphycical teachings of the ancients. In fact, even purely physical scientific discoveries could cost a man his head.

Over the years I "crossed paths" with other metaphysical students who recalled "crossing paths" with me in previous lives. Was this just interesting "coincidence?"

* Page 24.

‹ FRANÇAIS :

devoir
utres »

on prononcée par le
dio nationale

confiance, le salut de la
France, que mettraient
en danger nos discordes,
sera la récompense de
notre union. »

Les associations secrètes
seront dissoutes
ET LEURS BIENS MIS SOUS SÉQUESTRE

*Des peines sévères sont prévues pour les individus
qui tenteraient de reconstituer ces sociétés*

La loi portant interdiction des sociétés secrètes, publiée à l'« Officiel », et dont nous avons fait connaître hier l'économie générale, dispose que sont dissous de plein droit, à dater de la promulgation de la présente loi :

1° Toute association, tout groupement de fait, dont l'activité s'exerce, même partiellement, de façon clandestine ou secrète ;

2° Toute association, tout groupement de fait dont les affiliés s'imposent, d'une manière quelconque, l'obligation de cacher à l'autorité publique, même partiellement, les manifestations de leur activité ;

3° Toute association, tout groupement de fait qui refuse ou néglige de faire connaître à l'autorité publique, après en avoir été requis, ses statuts et règlements, organisation intérieure, sa hiérarchie, e de ses membres avec l'indication s charges qu'ils occupent, l'objet de ses réunions, ou qui fournit intentionnellement sur ce sujet des renseignements faux et incomplets.

La nullité des groupements ou associations visés ci-dessus est constatée par décret.

Les biens mobiliers et immobiliers de ces associations et groupements dissous seront, à la requête du ministère public, placés sous séquestre par ordonnance du président du tribunal civil du lieu de leur situation.

Il sera procédé à leur liquidation.

La loi dispose d'autre part que sera puni d'un emprisonnement de 6 mois à 2 ans et d'une amende de 16 à 5 000 francs quiconque aura participé au maintien ou à la reconstitution directe ou indirecte des associations ou groupements dissous.

L'OFFENSIVE AÉRIENNE
CONTRE L'ANGLETERRE
prend une ampleur accrue

Le D.N.B. apprend que de nouveaux avions allemands ont quitté de bonne heure leurs bases en Allemagne et en Belgique, le temps étant favorable pour de nouvelles opérations. Grâce aux nuages qui s'amoncelaient au-dessus de la Manche, les avions allemands ont pu atteindre la côte anglaise sans être remarqués.

LE BILAN DES PERTES

Les pertes totales de l'adversaire pour une seule journée sont de 132 avions et de 12 ballons d[e] barrage, dont 80 avions abatt[us] dans des combats aériens et [au] sol et par la D.C.A.

28 appareils alleman[ds] manquants.

Le ministre de l'[...] communique :

Dans la jour[...] 78 appareils e[...] abattus au co[...] se sont dér[...] l'Angleterr[...]

13 ap[...] manqu[...] tes or[...]

[...] canon de 32 m de long
[...]eint l'Angleterre depuis Calais

[...]a ajoute que malgré l'absence de communications officielles de la part de la Grande-Bretagne, on apprend que deux localités ont été atteintes, situées sur la côte sud-orientale de l'île.

La première action des canons a été déclenchée au cours de la matinée et a duré une demi-heure. Elle a été reprise par la suite. Dans les deux cas, le feu de l'artillerie se poursuivit pendant l'action des bombardements aériens et du survol par les avions allemands, ce qui donne à supposer que le tir était réglé d'après les indications fournies par les avions.

[...] TIRÉ
[...] FOIS
[...]GLAISES

[...] italienne dif[...]aivante :

[...]dances datées de [...]llées par les jour[...] York confirment la nouvelle [...]après laquelle des projectiles d'artillerie sont tombés sur le territoire anglais.

Lond[...]

Another example of a group of Parallel People - all quite unaware of this fact - college students who landed at the same table at a wedding feast, adjoining mine. I noticed, or felt, there seemed to be something special about this group. When I asked one friendly young man for his birthday, it turned out to be an exact trine to mine, so I asked the others and found that 7 out of 9 were born in Fire Signs Sidereally, also, 6 within 10 degrees of each other. This is another illustration of "birds of a feather" alighting together. Synchronicity? Would a follow up reveal any more synchronicity in their future lives?

To quote Carl G. Jung, "Synchronicity is an acausal connecting principle."

I tried to follow up on the student group and was even more amazed to learn 2 more students had been invited who had not shown up - but were also born in Fire Signs, and within 5 degrees of the first group, bringing the total to 9 out of 11!

There are several ways in which one can observe the well-oiled clockwork of ongoing creation.

The group encountered at that wedding party again called my attention to the concentration of initimate friends and family born during the third decade of December. Here they are for me, in addition to the above mentioned special group:

December 19th—2
December 20th—1
December 21st—1
December 23rd—3
December 24th—5
December 25th—3
December 26th—1
December 27th—1
December 28th—2

You will find it interesting to observe and record the birthdays of your friends and relatives.

If, indeed, we meet people again in subsequent incarnations, as many regressions seem to indicate, this should express itself in figures. I started to collect birthdays of people I seemed to harmonize with particularly well. I found results quite different from what popular astrology proclaims. (1) My findings did not agree with the popular "Sun" signs of people, or even with their sidereal signs. (2) I got results much more striking if I examined just a few days, in this instance more specifically the last decade of December. There was a general group from the 17th to the 30th with an inner group from the 19th to the 26th, almost exactly one week. *These* were the people I almost always "clicked" with instantly, or almost immediately reached meaningful communication. Astrologers would say that they are in "TRINE" with my "Natal Sun" on August 20th. I like to theorize that their orbits are running parallel and therefore meet again and again in the Cosmic Ocean.

Try your own list of relatives, friends, lovers, children, and tell me what you find. I reported some of my findings in the SIDEREALIST Magazine No. 5 of 1980.

JIM MARBERRY'S STORY

I was all set to play golf but I needed someone to play with. Bill, the golf-starter, like many who have dealt with the public for a long time had lost some of his sensitivity. "Here comes Jim," he said, "He's weird enough to play with anyone!"

"Hurry up!" he shouted to me, "Catch those 3 Japs headed for Tee One. They can't speak a word of English!"

I sprinted for the number One Tee.

Playing golf with my 3 Japanese partners was a new experience. Whoever coined the phrase: "Shoot a round of golf," had them in mind. It was hit and run, with no particular regard for any niceties such as safety or etiquette.

After 3 holes, there was no one behind us, so on Tee 4 I decided to tarry awhile and help one of my partners find a lost ball. What then unfolded is one of the most amazing experiences of my life. I was startled by his first question:

"How old you?"

"45."

"Birthday?"

"November 16th."

"You in war?"

"Captain in Infantry, Chemical Warfare."

"All me too." he said.

As our golf game continued, so did our quest. Making adjustments for time changes and International Date Line, it appeared my Japanese friend and I were born at the SAME TIME. I was born in the town of Carbondale, Illinois, on the Mississippi Rover. He was born in the town of Sakai in the same size prefecture of Ibaraki, on the River Tone.

His family name was Yamanchi, mine Marberry, same number of letters. We were married at the same time. We both attended school in Pre-Med then switched to Chemistry. Our children were born at the same time. Both our youngest daughters died at the same age. We had the same number of children. We were both athletes and ended up as teachers. We both played golf and the day we met we were both wearing black golfing sweaters. We met at the Golf Club in Alameda. During our military service in World War II we both remained in our home countries, did not go overseas.

Through my acceptance of others, I had received a great reward - I had met my "double."

On the conclusion of our golf game, I invited my 3 Japanese friends to my home to socialize, but mainly to continue the quest into the many parallels of our lives. My son John and I went to their ship for dinner and for the evening, which was spent in pursuit of earthly identities, thumbing through the Japanese-English Dictionary to validate any doubts.

All the startling parallels of our lives seemingly had to do with the fact that we had been born at the same time. Was it true that our lives were pre-destined? Were we compelled to act in the way we did? I decided to defy fate and take charge of my life, to become self-sufficient and independent. I made changes in my life, important changes, which took courage and a strong belief in myself to attempt this decision making.

I would be very interested in knowing if my Japanese-parallel and I have continued to have similar experiences in view of my assertive control of my life. Is he also where I am at now?

Chapter III
Centuries of Delays

The reason why not much research was done until this century in the field of metaphysical studies was that it was beyond the pale of studies permitted by the self-appointed and anointed expert authorities of the scientific and political establishments, also in close alliance with the latter, the orthodox churches.

All of these well established groups felt threatened by new ideas that were unfamiliar to them, and in which they could therefore not automatically usurp the leadership which in most fields had been conceded to them by unthinking traditional habits of custom. This was basically a struggle for the consumer's dollars, drachmae or shekels or denarii, through the churches' or temples' monopoly of sale of indulgences and sacraments. This meant for them income as well as maintenance of tax-free properties, and other privileges, granted them by the kings and princes - if they promised to use their knowledge exclusively for the benefit of such members of the ruling classes. Of course, they did not like any competition from free-thinking philosophers.

There was the secondary reason that a little knowledge is really dangerous - dangerous for "the sorcerer's apprentice," as we are apt to call it today, or dangerous also for the rest of us when an inexperienced workman pulls the wrong switch at a nuclear power plant! It does not have to be a terrorist with a bomb. Much smaller things canbe disastrous enough! So it was throughout history. This is the main reason why the great teachers of all kinds, physical as well as metaphysical, gave out their knowledge to their pupils only by the teaspoon, while concurrently testing their character.

In addition to their endangering themselves, as well as other people, there was also the political aspect of the sacred teachings. The holders of other well ingrained opinions do not hesitate to go to extremes to prevent new ideas from being propagated. Many were the martyrs in science. Nowadays, independent thinkers are not apt to be burnt at the stake, like Giordano Bruno was, as late as 1600, after 6 years of torture - a fate that Galileo himself barely escaped. He had adopted Copernicus' idea of displacing the earth from the central position which had been attributed to it by Ptolemaeus, and this threatened the earth-centered philosophy of the church. This meant displacing the church from its position as central control tower of humanity. Thus the mysteries of the universe were open to searching minds.

There is really no conflict between religious thinking and reincarnation. For it has been part of most religions from time immemorial. The Egyptians elaborated on it, and it was in Egypt that it entered into the thinking of the Hebrews. There should not be any more objection to obsrving the Creator's clockwork than to reading the hands of an ordinary clock with several dials. But we have to remember that not more than a few hundred years ago it was a *capital* offense to affirm that the earth was a sphere, and that it revolved around the sun - known facts today and commonly accepted.

It seems strange to an astrologer that astrology is still a blasphemous taboo for many of the organized churches. Others, it is true, do not see any conflict, but the ones whose very livelihood depends on complete mental control over their adherents are deadly afraid of the consequences. If any of their followers were to try doing some independent thinking in this field, they might think on other subjects, too. Some might even be tempted to seek to make direct contacts with the Creator. This would by pass confession and other profitable sacraments. If today many people are taking an interest in reincarnation, it is possible only due to the loosening of the mental ties that for centuries have bound them to their churches. If these churches are losing adherents constantly, it is largely due to their trying to dominate the thinking of slowly maturing humanity, which starts rebelling against such treatment.

Belief in reincarnation was officially proscribed at the Second Council of Constantinople, in 553 A.D.

Christian references to reincarnation include some of the best known Catholic writers, such as:

Eusebius, Bishop of Caesarea, author of the Caesarean Creed, later Bishop of Constantinople, whose writings are still a chief source of church history up to 324 A.D.

Saint Augustine, best known through his "Confessions," internationally famed scholar and Bishop of Hippo in Roman Africa. He was a philosopher deeply influenced by Plotinus whom he studied thoroughly while still a pagan - before his conversion to Christianity. He later became an outstanding influence in the Church. In his "Confessions" (I:6) he asks: "Did I not live in another body before entering my mother's womb?"

Saint Augustine also wrote in his "Contra Academia," "Plotinus, a Platonist, so like his master ... one would think Plato is born again in Plotinus."

If one studies the writings of Saint Augustine and Saint Eusebius, one might well come to the conclusion that all the essential elements of the Christian religions had already existed in various parts of the world of the Antique, at least a thousand years before Jesus.

Thus, Zarathustra, Buddha, Plato, and of course Moses, could be considered forerunners of Jesus, and his appearance at the time in history when it occurred could be considered as a reincarnation of their ideas and ideals and those of the teachers that preceded them, particularly in India where the golden rule and the commandments were already in force long before. The "second coming" now would also be a logical sequel as a new reincarnation.

Clement of Alexandria said that reincarnation was a truth, and authorized by Saint Paul himself.

Some of the sects of Christianity which taught rebirth were the Gnostics, Manichaeans, Albigensians, Priscillianists. Protestantism did not bring about spiritual freedom. The reformers were puritanical themselves and became more orthodox than the Church which they condemned. Of course, theirs was only lip-service, as the well known divorces of King Henry VIII and Luther's patron, the Prince of Hessen, demonstrated. They were even probably one of the main, underlying reasons why the Reformation became possible.

The Pope would not allow divorces, but the princes did not really care whether he approved of them or not, although excommunication would not have strengthened their position. They felt a lot more secure on their thrones with the moral approval of their subjects. This is called "religious reinsurance." Their answer was to change "the moral standards."

So they were willing to help to create new "protestant" church organizations and made their subjects follow the new religion. They did reap a few fringe benefits by cutting loose from the Pope. They could control not only the appointments of new church dignitaries, confiscate the church properties and then could tax them as well, and so the monies from the new churches would benefit them rather than go to Rome, where the objectionable "indulgences" had of course flowed as well.

Reincarnation has been proven scientifically in quite a few well documented cases, but has it been "proved" that the "dead" are dead for good? On the contrary, some kind of a resurrection or belief in eternal life forms part of most religions.

Has it been "proved" that souls go to "heaven" after "death"? Or that souls go to "hell" after "death"?

Saint Gregory of Nyssa: "The soul needs to be purified, and if this does not take place during this life on earth, it must be accomplished in future lives."

Reincarnation also appears in the Bible, in numerous places, always mentioned in a very casual manner, as a matter of course, and never subject to question or to dispute, just discussion - not only in the Old Testament, where Isaiah and Maleachi prophesied the coming back of Elijah as a forerunner to the Messiah, but also in the Jewish sacred writings, particularly the Zohar and Cabbalah in great detail.

The Talmud states that the soul of Abel passed into the body of Seth and from that into the body of Moses. Cain was reincarnated as the Egyptian that was slain by Moses, thus paying the karma of his previous evil action.

In the New Testament we have numerous references to rebirths. 3 are quoted and more listed: *

Matthew XI:7-14

When John's disciples had gone, Jesus began talking about him to the crowds. "When you went out into the barren wilderness to see John, what did you expect him to be like? Grass blowing in the wind? Or were you expecting to see a man dressed as a prince in a palace? Or a prophet of God? Yes, and he is more than just a prophet. For John is the man mentioned in the Scriptures - a messenger to precede me, to announce my coming, and prepare people to receive me.

"Truly, of all men ever born, none shines more brightly than John the Baptist. And yet, even the lesser lights in the Kingdom of Heaven will be greater than he is! And from the time John the Baptist began preaching and baptizing until now, ardent multitudes have been crowding toward the Kingdom of Heaven, for all the laws and prophets looked forward (to the Messiah). Then John appeared, and if you are willing to understand what I mean, he is Elijah, the one the prophets said would come (at the time the Kindgom begins)."

Matthew XVII:10-13

His disciples asked, "Why do the Jewish leaders insist Elijah must return before the Messiah comes?" Jesus replied, "They are right. Elijah must come and set everything in order. And, in fact, he has already come, but he wasn't recognized, and was badly mistreated by many. And I, the Messiah, shall also suffer at their hands." Then the disciples realized he was speaking of John the Baptist.

I Corinthians XV:42-44

In the same way, our earthly bodies which die and decay are different from the bodies we shall have when we come back to life again, for they will never die. The bodies we have now embarrass us for they become sick and die, but they will be full of glory when we come back to life again. Yes, they are weak, dying bodies now, but when we live again they will be superhuman bodies. For just as there are natural, human bodies, there are also supernatural, spiritual bodies.

In regard to the reality of a future life, there are many Biblical quotations supporting this fact: to cite just a few:

II Kings - II—11,
Psalms - XC: 1 & 15,
Proverbs - VIII: 22 to 31, XXII:1,
Ecclesiasts - IX: 5 and 6
Jeremiah - I:5,
Malachi - I:2 and 3, IV: 5,
Wisdom Solomon's - VIII: 19 and 20,

---

*Quotations from "The Living Bible," Billy Graham Crusade edition.

Matthew - IV:14, XI—10, XIV: 1 and 2, XVI: 13 and 14,
XVII: 11 to 13, XXVIII: 9.
Mark - VI: 15 and 16, VIII: 27 and 28, IX: 9-13, XI:28,
Luke - IX: 7-9, IX: 18-19, I: 17,
John - VIII: 5-8, IX: 1-3, XX: 15, XXI:4,
Acts - I:9,
Romans - IX: 10-13,
I Corinthians - XV: 42-44,
Revelation - III: 12.

It should not be lost sight of that these references still remained in the Bible after it had been expurgated several times by orthdox churchmen, who feared that the knowledge of reincarnation might cause undesirable thoughts of independence in their flock - such as the idea of praying and communicating directly with the deity, instead of having to pay indulgence fees to the priests.

At one time, the idea of reincarnation received an almost fatal blow - when an Empress of Byzantium insisted on its being expurgated from the official Christian teachings because it would, she thought, undermine her imperial authority in that it would give the common people the idea that SHE might have been a *slave* in a former life, or worse, that she might be reduced to that state IN HER NEXT LIFE, and thus give them the fatal idea of *equality!*

To quote Helen Blavatsky, "Universal TRUTH has been sacrificed to the insane conceit of little men."

Chapter IV
My Initiation Into Reincarnation

I had a sudden, striking personal experience which stimulated my interest in the subject of reincarnation. I had heard about it in a very general manner, from Pythagoras and the works of Plato, also the Gospels of Saint Matthew, Saint Luke, Saint Mark, Saint John, Saint Augustine - but had looked at it from "the outside" as one might say and was not concerned with it in a personal way.

Then, one day in Paris, in 1932 ... I had just been transferred from the New York Head Office to Paris, as Assistant Manager of the European HQ of a multi-national US corporation, and we were waiting for our new apartment on St. Cloud Heights to be finished. We stayed for several months in a very small hotel - old fashioned but comfortable - the Hotel Cambon on the Rue Cambon near the Louvre Gardens. One evening we went from our 3rd floor room to the 4th floor where we had been invited by an elderly American lady for a visit.

We had a glass of wine and talked about Paris, and about the good food they served in the hotel. Then our hostess offered us a stronger drink in about a 2-ounce glass. Unsuspecting, keeping up with the speed of the wine drinking, I drank about half in one gulp, and burst out with: "Are you trying to poison me AGAIN?"

To this, she replied in the most natural manner: "Well, I think you amply deserved it!"

"What did I do?"

"You were responsible for my husband being sentenced to the sulphur mines near Agrigentum."

Time spun back for me some 700 years. I recalled the scene where I rode into a castle high up in the hills of central Sicily, and after the hot ride asked for a drink. As I accepted the proferred drink my horse shied and I dropped the beaker to seize the reins. In this instant I knew I was to have been poisoned. My groom sniffed: "Cyanide."

I had not realized who the lady was, but I had come to her castle after her husband's arrest to see about some legal matters, being District Attorney for the Royal Government of the French Norman d'Hauteville dynasty recently merged, in the person of the infant Frederic II with the German imperial dynasty of the Hohenstaufen. I remembered her only after she recognized me. It was just one of a hundred legal cases for me. I was so shocked that I failed to ask her for her name in Sicily, and I forgot her name in this life. However, I never saw her again. The event seemed to have an incisive and lasting effect on our relations. I don't remember the outcome of the incident in Sicily. She obviously wanted revenge, even at the risk of her life.

In the following years, in different localities, in Europe and America, I met 3 other women who seemed to recognize me and to dislike me. Several of them spoke specifically and in detail about my deeds against their husbands in that same past life. It all seemed to fit in with my job in Sicily when I was obligated to handle many such cases. It appears to me that hatred is more lasting than love. However, I have made contact with children of mine from those days - a son Alexander and a daughter Beatrice for whom I do have feelings of love. I have been asked: "Did you not meet the mother of your children?" The answer is that I did, and there was mutual recognition, but also immediate agreement to let the past remain in the past - peaceful but total detachment. Requiescat in Pace.

I must affirm that these spontaneous personal recalls, that other people had, convinced me more than the teaching of Plato or the Gospel according to St. Matthew.

So did my father's time-dated poems.

Here was something recorded in black and white, within my own lifetime - something tangible, if poetry can be called such.

It is generally agreed that poetry lifts the consciousness to a higher level. It seemed to be up to me to demonstrte this. My father's specimens were convincing. You will find one in Chapter V.

Poems are probably the purest form of spontaneous recollections. I shall present some later, and some quotations from third parties, as well as experiences of friends.

We may have our doubts about people remembering only pomp and glory in their past lives, rather than existences as humble laborers in the vineyard. Upon due reflection, however, we realize that we are all more apt to remember the more exiciting experiences whether good or bad then humdrum average lives. Are we not more likely to remember a wonderful vacation in Hawaii than the one when we decided to spend our 2 weeks at home painting the house?

One who reports a past life as a prominent public servant may be accused of boasting and is regarded with jealousy by those for whom such an experience is still in the future. Let me assure you, it is no bed of roses.

I feel that all entities will have to go through lifetimes on a great variety of levels and qualities, as only in that manner can one look at life from vastly differing points of view, and thus in life-after-life experience all facets of life-on-earth.

Personally, I have had experiences on the lowest social levels as well as on fairly high ones. I was a black slave in early Egypt, a Jew in hostile Hellenistic Egypt, a blonde hooker in France, was stoned as a heretic in Flanders, was a teacher on Rhodes, a student under Poseidonios. 500 years earlier I was a Greek sailor in the colonisation of Krotona and Poseidonia in Magna Graecia. I was a politically exposed attorney-general in Sicily and again 300 years later a writer in Sicily. I was a poet in several incarnations.

So I have come a long way -- but I feel sure the diamond of my soul still has quite a few additional facets to be ground by the emery wheels of life to become beautiful as well as useful from all points of view.

I have never been a King or a Queen - yet!

I could go for being a Space-Man, or a scientist. Best of all I would like to establish and/or operate a Center for artists, writers, philosophers, in beautiful surroundings, especially in Latin America like my mentor, Professor E. B. Szekely did in Costa Rica.

Chapter V
Time Tables

As to the WHEN and HOW of the TIME TABLES of The Cosmic Clocks, the great minds of the past and the present vary considerably. Many teach there is an average of 144 years between incarnations. Some outstanding teachers, such as Manly P. Hall, Madame Blavatsky and Max Heindel, talk about periods averaging 1000 years between incarnations, some even 1500 years, or more. Also, there is considerable evidence of cases with almost immediate rebirths, particularly with martyrs or deaths in battle.

Such long intervals between reappearances might make sense if we compare the hypothetical orbits of such exceptional entities to the hyperbolic tracks of comets. Both types of orbits could thus very well co-exist.

We are not really sure of the durations of the cycles, but the 1000-year intermissions seems too long to check on them effectively. Therefore, it seemed best to start with those a little more accessible to investigation, such as an 150 year average, or 144 year average. So far, we find the 144 year cycle the one giving the most tangible results. It is the cycle preferred by The Ancient Mystical Order Rosai Crucis "AMORC" It is probably not infallible but it seems to work out in average practice, while the 1000 year cycle of other groups is almost exactly 7 cycles of 144 years.

When I first heard about the 144 year cycle I was very interested, but being a skeptic and a student of Cartesius I decided to put this idea to a test. It would have to be an independent test, not something into which my personal fancy or imagination could enter, nor that of anybody whom I might influence by my interest in the subject. How could I do that?

Finally, it occurred to me that I had a perfect example just under my nose - my father's poems! His poems had always impressed me by their vivid descriptions of certain specific historical events. One particular poem however had puzzled me with his vivid decription of the siege of Weinsberg in the Peasants' War (1525). It was written from a woman's point of view! By my father?

Well, I learned when I began to study the subject of reincarnation that it is a regular feature of the system that the sex of the reincarnating soul, or entity, changes from time to time, though not necessarily from one life to the next.

Now the veil slid from my eyes: my father must have been one of the women who saved their husbands' lives by backpacking them out of the surrendering city at the last minute in big wicker baskets. They were permitted to take out their most valued possessions, but only what they could carry on their backs! This was almost exactly 3 x 144 years ago, from the date of his poem. My puzzlement was solved.

Another outstanding event was the Battle of Cannae, of which my father had written an incredibly vivid description 2100 years later! It was so vivid, so full of feeling, so strong, that it seemed it just might have been written by a participant - more than just an observer, that was sure. He was not killed in the battle. He described it with details to the very tragic end, and beyond that into the very night. Because of his being an aged bard, he must have been one of the lucky ones, one of the very few Roman prisoners the Carthaginians took on that day in June, 216 B.C. I went to my calculator: it was almost exactly 15 x 144 years. I was convinced.

I am including my translation of my father's poem. Perhaps it will not render the poetical quality, but I hope I have at least transposed the impact of the feeling of the poem. (On next 3 pages).

Der Abend von Cannä
(Juni 216 v. Chr.)

Wie die Abgottschlange die Ringe preßt
Um den stampfenden Stier und nicht los ihn läßt,
Bis die Rippen des Riesen krachen,
So wand um die Römer den töblichen Ring
Des karthagischen Heerwurms schillernd Geschling,
Bis erstickt sie erlagen dem Drachen.

Da sanken dahin sie in Staub und Blut
In der Junisonne vernichtender Glut,
Die Reiter und Legionare.
Es türmten zu Haufen die Toten sich
Und schlossen zu Wällen sich fürchterlich
Um die Konsuln und Konsulare.

— In Strömen das römische Blut verrinnt,
Und die glänzenden Waffen, sie werden blind
Wie die Augen, die sterbend brechen.
Des Aufidus Wellen geh'n purpurrot,
Und über das Schlachtfeld jagt hetzend der Tod
Seine Numiderhunde, die frechen.

Die spüren das Leben, wo es noch stöhnt,
Und wissen, wie man noch den Sterbenden höhnt,
Eh' der Dolch ihm die Kehle durchschneidet.
Sie zerren den Ring von erstarrender Hand
Und reißen vom blutigen Leib das Gewand
Und lassen ihn liegen entkleidet.

— Und über der nackten Leiber Schwall
Auf fahlem Roß reitet Hannibal,
Sein grimmiges Einauge funkelt. —
Und hinter dem Feldherrn schreitet die Nacht,
Aufflammen die Feuer der punischen Wacht;
Der Abend von Cannä dunkelt. —

Theo Endemann
1920

THE BATTLE OF CANNAE (216 B.C.)

As the Anaconda tightens its rings
Around the stamping bull, and does not let go
Until it has cracked his ribs,
The Carthaginian army's glittering host
Wound deadly rings 'round the Roman troops
Until, smothered, they fell to the Dragon.

In the June sun's withering heat they sank.
They fell into blood and dust and sand,
The knights, the horsemen and legionnaires.
Their corpses piled up into walls of dread
'Round the consuls and consularians.
Their glittering arms turned dim and dull
As their eyes dimmed, faded in dying.

The Roman blood ran off in streams
To the river, gleaming like purple -
Now death chases over the battlefield,
Its bloodhounds: impudent Numidians.
They scent any life that still flickering moans,
Know how to mock the dying's last groans,
Ere the dagger cuts their quivering throats.
They tear the ring from the stiffening hand,
Drag the tunics from bleeding corpses,
Leaving them lying naked, like worms.

And over the naked corpses wall
On his fellow steed, here comes Hannibal,
Trampling all under his horse's hooves -
His one eye ferociously flashing.

Behind the victorious Commander in Chief
Lurk slinking the shadows of night;
Soon flicker Phoenician Guards' campfire lights.
Over Cannae rises the night tide.

Now, as I have a Pisces Ascendant, which gives me the inclination to write poems, and Neptune as leader of the pack of my planets (the first planet to appear after the Ascendant in the natal chart), all this apparently makes me also a bit too flexible to be orderly and precise. As a consequence of this, I am afraid I shall have to go through a hard school of precision and orderliness the next time around, in other words - as a Virgo man. I believe it is harder on a man to be a Virgo, so I'll probably get that problem as a monkey on my back. I will hope for a better chance as a Libra dancing-girl the next round after that!

Some writers seem to favor the idea of reincarnations progressing counter-clockwise through the Zodiac, but I could not pinpoint where I originally encountered this theory, which does seem to be confirmed in my personal experience.

A suicide may be compared to a "drop-out." There simply will be unfinished work to be done in another life time. It does not change the programming of the University of Life, it does not enable anyone to obtain diplomas, it simply automatically grants a dishonorable discharge.

A suicide interferes with the time tables; it is contrary to natural law. Socrates chose to be executed according to the law of the land, rather than compromise on principles. Many Christian martyrs followed the same principle. Generally, suicides are most prevalent during climacterial years.

As Manly P. Hall puts it: "A suicide's karma he automatically stacks so that in a future incarnation he will die under conditions where his desire to live will be greatest."

He may also be reborn almost immediately and programmed for repeats and for additional subjects. There seems to be agreement that sudden death such as in battle, or by accident, may involve a return almost immediately, to complete the "assignment."

On the other hand, if Pythagoras or Plato should not come back for 1000 or 1500 years, as some claim, this would disrupt the Law of Equality, of Cause and Effect. If there is a law, it should not disavow itself. Should advanced spirits ask for special privileges or exceptions?

Philosophers speak of liberation from the Wheel of Life in a general way, to be attained by self-perfection under the Law of Cause and Effect. Those who do NOT *have* to come back constitute the teachers, anxious to reach down from the other side to help those on the ladder. Of course, actually we know little about and have proven nothing of all these theories.

Pherecydes of Syros, as reported by Pindar, envisages only "3 lives on this side" and "3 on the other" and after that "perfect bliss." Opinions or ideas on what that might be are divided.

Poseidonios describes it as gazing at the clear sky and understanding it.

Virgil puts it this way: "Happiness will be to understand the way of the stars, to know the reason for the eclipses and earthquakes and tides. These were the desires which the disembodied souls in the upper world satisfied to their heart's content." Virgil says:

"Felix qui potuit rerum cognoscere causas."

(Happy is he who understands the causes of things.)

I must say that such research satisfies me also, more than anything else I can think of - to watch the Cosmic Clocks, that ring up the works of the Creator.

Yes, happy is he who understands the causes (and reasons) for what happens, and therefore understands eternal justice and finds it easy to accept it.

The Christian way of expressing the same thought is: "attunement with the will of God." If one understands the big "whys" and "hows" one feels at peace with oneself and the world, because it makes sense and therefore is not difficult to fall in with. Justice IS.

PROGRESSIONS OF REINCARNATIONS

Since the question of "correctional facilities" hardly seems to lend itself to verification by computer, we may never - in time or space - know where our next classes will be held, when we do not get "passing" grades at the end of our present "term," and are condemned to take the same lessons over again.

Not having been able to find anything tangible, or even much intangible matter, on this subject, I can only admit that the idea of rotating classrooms appeals to me; and I can quite well see myself as having been a Cancer female in my last previous life, even to the point of using symbolical claws as a hooker. This would also explain my strangely deep sympathy for the members of this profession, amazingly combined with a complete lack of interest in their services.

This I had excellent opportunity to observe during my long years in Paris where probably the best quality in this category was available, and where it was frequently offered to me for free on the expense accounts of visiting firemen (Presidents and Vice-Presidents of American companies) who were amazed at my polite refusals ... of such generous offers.

In my present life I am considered to be a typical Leo, even my computer friends admit this. I am actually a Leo under both the currently popular Greek Zodiac, better known as the Tropical Zodiac, as well as under the ancient Sidereal Zodiac of the Chaldeans (and Egyptians and Hindus). In our research we seem to have found that people who have the same constellations on Ascendcant and Midheaven and Sun sign under both zodiacs are frequently "test book cases" fitting the descriptions in conventional astrological literature.

ARE THERE GENIUS VINTAGES?

An interesting study has been made by Edward Lyndoe which he reported in American Astrology, August 1980 (page 13). He notes what he calls "a boosting of Genius" every 72 years, which corresponds to every second Saturn-Neptune conjunction. The striking thing seems to be that only every other conjunction appears to bring that extra crop of genius babies. We shall have to look for the outside factor which is missing on the 36 year conjunction. Boom years were 1809 and 1882. It is too early to judge the conjunction by the results of the 1952 crop.

What is particularly interesting is that the period of 72 years is exactly one-half a hypothetical reincarnational cycle of an average of 144 years. Could it be that there was also an intermission, an average "resting period" of 72 years involved? Much has been said about such periods of rest or waiting, but nothing concrete is known, although it is an interesting theory and worthwhile studying.

Lyndoe notes that at the intermediate 36-year conjunction very little seems to happen in the way of special births. There are some outstanding people born, but very few in comparison to the 72 year cycle.

An important interval seems to be involved also in the old traditional "three score and ten." Could it be possibly more precisely "three score plus a dozen," or simpler "six dozen years?" I prefer it as 70, or 10 times the general normal earth period of 7 years.

When the terrestrial cycle of 7 years and the spiritual and sidereal cycle of 12 years are combined at 84 year intervls, many mental peaks are reached when approaching that conjunction and sometimes beyond that. Outstanding examples are Goethe, Franklin, Tolstoy, Churchill, Kerensky, Somerset Maugham, Adenauer, Michelangelo, Pablo Casals, Pablo Picasso, Albert Schweitzer, Mary Baker Eddy, George Bernard Shaw, Bertrand Russell.

Chapter VI
Languages

It seems possible that I may have inherited some language ability through the genes of my ancestors. My great-grandfather Wenck started to learn English a hundred years ago at the age of 65, when it became apparent that it would be beneficial for his business. He was selling foundry supplies to England.

All my Endemann ancestors, since at least 1600 A.D., were professionally obliged to master a minimum of 4 languages: German, Latin, Greek and Hebrew, for their work as Protestant bishops. Several of them probably studied Aramaic as well — for Biblical study — and some French for general education.

On my father's mother's side we also had several consecutive generations of Hugenot pastors as ancestors, which meant constant exposure to at least Latin and Greek. I am not sure of the requirements of Hebrew there. Now all this Latin practice on the part of my ancestors for over 3 centuries may explain why in this life I was able to enjoy indulging in "lingual acrobatics"*, as Professor E.B. Szekely dubbed it; and further that surprisingly my "acrobatics" were able to stand up under close scrutiny by professional Latin scholars 30 years after I had left school and discontinued the study of Latin. I remember that the study of Latin in school was so boringly easy for me that I did my homework for other subjects that were harder for me, such as mathematics or science, under the table. Latin came to me easily, as did Dutch conversation and French irregular verbs.

However, this does not explain, at least to MY satisfaction, my personal affinity for other quite unrelated languages, which transpired later and which had made me believe I must have lived on this earth before, more than just once or twice.

Although I seemed to have always had an above-average facility for learning languages, in time it became apparent to me that there was a great difference in my facility for learning one language or another.

German was my native language. In those days anybody who claimed to have an education had to know French. This was so ever since the days of Frederic the Great. My first French teacher was excellent. He made it interesting to learn French with good and attractive textbooks, and his own flawless pronunciation. He was mobilized in World War I and we had another teacher who did not really master the language, and who tried to force me into dead, textbook grammar. Feeling an intense affinity for everything French, I had by that time read every French book I could get hold of, including most of Victor Hugo, Zola, Dumas and some more modern writers. I confronted him with quotations from modern literature when he tried to correct my themes. It never occurred to me at that time that this was a somewhat extraordinary situation. When I was in France for a week, en route to the USA, I felt immediately at home, thanks to my first French teacher, Professor Ludewig, but many years later I realized there was much more to it than having a good teacher and good textbooks.

In the meantime I had added a third language to my repertoire — Latin. Next came Greek, but to my regret after a good start my family moved and we did not find another teacher. At the "REAL GYMNASIUM" (high school) my fifth language was English. We had a very good teacher who had just returned to Germany from several years training at Oxford. When we were ready for finals, he told us that we could spell better than the same age youths in England. We thought he just wanted to pat himself on the back, but the time came when I realized how true his statement had been. Dr. Stier had really drilled it into us on the basis of British historian Thomas B. Macaulay's *History of England,* as well as modern writers: J.K. Jerome, Joseph Conrad, Robert Louis Stevenson, Sir Walter Scott, and Jack London.

VOYAGE TO GONDWANA pages 26, 27.

LANGUAGES RECALLED

Very interesting to me has been the theory that one may trace an incarnation genetically by an accent that may not be reasonably or logically accounted for in one's current lifetime. I now speak German with a slight American accent, and American with a slight German, and noticeable French accent, with a dash of Scottish (which rubbed off from a Scottish wife of some 20 years). This is all reasonably explained from my whereabouts, BUT my French accent is not so easily explained. I spent most of my 13 years in France in Paris, but my accent is decidedly of the north of France, definitely not the expected Alsatian nor even Parisien. How come? If it is true that I was born, as I assume, in Lille near the end of the 18th century, this would be one explanation, and I tend to favor it.

My experience with the Russian language fits this kind of explanation, and is difficult to understand otherwise. I was interested in this language because it was different from the western European languages that I was familiar with, or so I thought until I took about 20 lessons in Russian from a highly educated Azerbeidjanian friend in Paris. I soon discovered that besides the Greek type alphabet (which I knew from my fourth language) there was a Greek type grammar, and a complete set of Holland Dutch abstract nouns (directly imported, with scientists, ship-builders, captains and all, by Czar Peter the Great from his study period as a shipbuilder in Holland. Finally a Viking vocabulary corresponding closely to the role of the Saxon vocabulary in English! All these made it easier for me to learn a little Russian, based on my knowledge of Greek, Dutch and Swedish.

The punch-line of all this was the mystery of my good accent in Russian, good enough that none of my Russian friends would believe I had had only a few lessons. Of course, I was far from mastering the language! There are many Russian people living in the area I live in and sometimes I cannot resist tossing a little Russian around, to which they respond in rapid-fire Russian, and I cannot follow. They expect me to know the language, after hearing me pronounce a few sentences. The explanation?

I did not have to learn how to pronounce it because Russian was my mother tongue in the middle of the 17th century north of the Caucasus, when I was a priest in a Kuban Cossack village.

English came after German, French, Latin and Greek, so was actually fifth in line. I do not recall any incarnation in this language. After leaving school, I started to study Spanish for about 20 lessons. I found it very easy to understand because of my familiarity with Latin, but I never achieved great efficiency in it. However, in spite of my broken Spanish during waking hours, strangely, I spoke fluent and perfect Spanish in my dreams. Where I picked that up I do not know. Perhaps I visited Spain from Portugal during the 15th and 16th centuries.

Holland Dutch, or Flemish, I picked up in the early 1920s as Amsterdam Branch Manager of a Hamburg Insurance Firm. It came to me easier than any other language ever. It came to me almost automatically within two or three months. I found two explanations for that; maybe they are actually only one. (a) I had probably spoken it in the 14th and 15th centuries in Flanders, also in Rjssel in 1800. (b) It is the present form of expression of the "Ripuarian" Franks, the people inhabiting the mouths of the Rhine river, which I could have inherited genetically from my mother's father born in Wesel near the Dutch border. This theory I found confirmed, or at least supported, when in 1969 I was visiting in a very small village in central Franconia and could easily and completely communicate with several dirt farmers there. On the other hand, on the many visits I had made to my grandmother's place at the edge of the Saxon Lowlands where "Plattdeutsch" or "Lowland German" was spoken, I could never learn the villagers' speech, and even less understand it.

Similarly, on the Baltic Island, where I grew up, I could not get to understand "Pomeranian," the local dialect. Even worse, I could never learn to read the works of Fritz Reuter, the most famous writer in the "Plattdeutsch." My classmates thought this was rather disgraceful affectedness on my part, and considered me a "high-brow, High-German kid." I really was not; I just could not twist my tongue the right way.

Could this be due to my not having had any incarnations in the Saxon-speaking lowlands of Germany? Likewise, in no Anglo-Saxon country?

On the other hand, the dialect of Frankfurt, a high-German dialect, came easy to me and I still have an ear for and limited facility in it, although I spent only the first 4½ years of my life there.

Several teachers of Latin have expressed surprise at my faculty of "linguistic acrobatics" in that language. I do not doubt that I had at least 2 incarnations using that language, although one of them was probably bi-lingual in Asia Minor, Crete and Rhodos, and Roman-controlled Syria.

Later, in Sicily, I must have been at least quadrilingual (French, German, Latin and Sicilian), possibly even familiar with Toscan, which was gradually emerging as the standard Italian language. In Sicily, the crossroads of the ANTIQUE, and the entire Mediterranean World's multicultural melting pot, multilingualism was a practical necessity for a public official or any other public person, in those days and places. A good example for that was Antonio Veneziano, who lived 3 cycles later. He was a Sicilian with Venetian background, who not only spoke, but even wrote poetry in Latin, Spanish, Toscan (the developing Italian) and Sicilian.

I have been asked why I do not recall a complete sequence of incarnations. This bothered me for a while, I must say, until I realized we cannot even recall all events of our current lives, and therefore cannot be surprised that it is at least as difficult to remember all the old ones. I am now trying to remember details of my years in Ohio, New York, Amsterdam, Paris and Hamburg, just to be able to give my children the complete autobiography which they have asked me for. Even for events of this current incarnation (such as the dates of my wedding days) I have to dig out old papers, meditate and ask friends, etc. So one can surely be excused for gaps in a story of incarnations.

Obviously, some of them were not packed so full of exciting events as others. There would not be so many details to remember from the quiet life of a farmer or cabinet-maker, or the life of a person with a quiet and unassuming personality.

Talking to some friends about languages and reincarnation has already brought forth some experiences that others have had in this field, which does not seem to have been plowed very deeply so far.

Hearing these stories refreshed my memories too, and I have just come across a letter I wrote to my grandfather in French when I was 10 years old, after one year of studying French in Junior High School. Now, looking at it carefully, I found that there was only one mistake in it. I had used the Imperfect Subjunctive instead of the Present Subjunctive: "que j'ecrivisse" instead of "que j'ecrive." Today it looks to me as if I subconsciously wanted to show off that I was familiar with the more rare tense.

I do not recall much detail from my 2-3 lives as a sailor. I cannot pretend that I shipped on the "Argo" nor in Ulysses' crews (those exciting trips I probably *would* remember), but I sailed at least twice with Athenian colonizers to Magna Graecia, to Krotona and to Poseidonia.

"The Kimberley Story," on the following page, is a truly convincing story of a language remembered. It is told by one of my best personal friends.

THE KIMBERLEY STORY

From the time she started to talk, my great-grand-daughter, Kimberley, appeared to have great difficulty in pronouncing her words, and in consequence was rather a slow talker, although she certainly was alert and intelligent.

One day I was visiting at my daughter's home, and Kimberley was there. She was about 4 years old at that time and was still having difficulty with her words. As I sat and watched her trying to tell us something she had done, it occurred to me that while she was trying to use the English words she was placing her tongue as though she was speaking FRENCH! I mentioned this to my daughter as perhaps pertaining to Kim's difficulty in talking.

An expression of surprise came over my daughter's face and she said, "Why, I never thought of that, but it might explain what happened the other day. Kimberley was not paying any attention to what I was saying to her — absolutely no attention. It was just as though she didn't hear me. It made me furious. Finally, I became so exasperated I shouted at her in FRENCH, telling her what I wanted her to do, and to my complete amazement, she promptly got up and did exactly as I had asked her. However, I was not more amazed at her doing what I said, than I was at my having spoken to her in French!"

My daughter Heather and her granddaughter are very close. Heather has always felt that she and Kim were somehow mixed up in the French Revolution!

As told by Edith M. Rowe

BENEFITS FROM USING THIRD LANGUAGES

Looking back with the clarity of hind-sight, it seems to me as if in this present life-span I have been given the program to catch up on languges, since it has come about that I have written my books in English, in the process of which I got an education in that language — which was only my 5th language learned in school.

The importance of languages in the subconscious seems to emerge more and more clearly for me. The French and Russian tongue syndromes come out very strong in my personality. I feel an affinity for everyting French. It took me half a century to become aware of why. Even more than the people, I tuned in on the language which had been my native tongue the last time around. It is like tuning in on the radio a certain wave-length where the voice comes through clearly and without static that may disturb the reception on neighborning stations. That's why I felt so at-home in France the first time I set foot in it. Other people have told me they had similar feelings in some strange country.

My Russian incarnation is a bit farther back — 300 years — but I note more than average affinity for people speaking that language, even though my knowledge of the language is very limited. It could be said the melody reverberates in my mind and, though the words do not penetrate the veil of the centuries, the feeling remains.

Likewise, for things Chinese there is just some feeling left, along with half a dozen words, but a deep understanding and empathy of the some 100 minorities in China, 2 of which I had close contacts with.

To return to the French language, it has been extremely useful to me in this life, for instance — permitting me, an American of German birth to communicate with a Canadian of Lebanese extraction. It has helped in contacts with other nationalities when otherwise I would have had difficulty in communication, such as with 4 or 5 acquaintances from Eastern European countries who eventually became close friends, and several Francophone Africans. The common language gives a feeling of being able to tune in, perhaps even more so if it is not the native tongue of either one of the 2 speakers, since no prejudice in favor of one's own language can enter into the conversation as a disturbing or deflecting factor. A language in common eliminates cultural differences as well.

In the never ending, always controversial and sometimes violent discussions of Races, Nationalities and Genetic Physical and Mental Qualities, an entire group of other influences of human behavior seems to have been disregarded ... Languages! The incisive and sometimes decisive influence of langauges is self-evident, all around us, whether we look at Kurdistan or Quebec, Wales, Eskalduna, Catalonia or Frisia.

Strange to say, until the end of the Middle Ages, languages did not have as much of an influence on politics. Even religion was managed, often fairly successfully, according to the age-old rule of thumb: *Cuius regio, ejus religio.* ("Whose region, his religion.") In other words, the king's religion determined that of his subjects. Similarly the ruler's language was the principal factor, although under enlightened princes this was not too strictly enforced. Frederic the Great proclaimed the principle: "Let every one go to heaven in his own way." It was with the accelerated evolution of industry and long distance communications, and the development of national states, that languages became really a divisive factor. It had been in the interest of kings to rule by division, and to maintain and protect the various minorities for that purpose.

When control of most of the world passed into the hands of dictatorships of the majority (nicely called "democracy" or "rule of the people") this brought about new trouble. Whereas a king was most likely to be fluent in 3 or 4 of the languages of his subjects and thus could more properly understand their desires and needs, with good rapport, the demagogues of the new regime often had a hard time using even their own dialect correctly and developed a pronounced inferiority complex when it came to any other language, looking upon it with suspicion that any conversation between their subjects in a strange tongue might be directed against them, in other words: subversive.

One of the very few exceptions which prove the rule is the Swiss democracy with 3 languages plus several local idioms. However, it was already well established when the above mentioned fundamental changes in social and economical life of the modern world took place. China, with its roughly 100 minorities, has it a little easier, by having one common written language.

In the days of the Roman Empire, even through the Renaissance, the universal tie was the "lingua franca" — actually the language of the OLD Romans which had gradually evolved from the so-called "golden" or classical idiom of the republic and early empire into the "silver Latin" of the provinces. But as such it was still the universal means of communication between all clerics, administrators, scientists and any other people of education. They still felt they were Roman citizens, at least in spirit. "Civis Romanus sum." was the badge-of-honor bestowed upon all free men in the confines of the empire, and a very effective means it was to ensure the loyalty of hundreds of thousands of members of the numerous minorities throughout the Roman world. Being their common, but neutral, language, the Romans' Latin outlasted their empire by a thousand years, quite apart from the several reincarnations in the many Romance languages. It thus found itself anchored in the sub-conscious of hundreds of thousands of spiritual heirs. This spirit surfaced notably in the several renaissances, not only in Italy but also in many remnants of the Roman Empire, and though modified, in the colonies of the colonies such as North America, Australia and others, where it is even still visible in architecture.

If 2 people of 2 different nationalities converse in a third language, which is not the native tongue for either of them, it is a "new ball game" altogether.

The neutral language will filter out most influences of the 2 speakers' possibly conflicting customs, habits and other cultural, national and even racial prejudices. With numerous thought-benders thus out of the way, the 2 can concentrate on the facts untainted and untinted by the colored glasses that almost all of us wear most of the time, thus approaching that seldom reached ideal of meaningful communication, so important for human relations on all levels.

BENEFITS FROM USING THIRD LANGUAGES

will beprinted simultaneously in Europe in the literary quarterly *New Europe* published in Luxembourg, headquarters of the European Economic Community and in the United States in the Anthology of addresses delivered at the **Fifth World Congress of Poets** in San Francisco July 6/10th, 1981. Also in Canada.

costa portugal
mauretania el aret
montanna
Carena
Carena
africa
nubia
Regnelli
maretay amasar
libia
libiamteior
mub
pentapoli
Camar
Affrica
montegilelli
Ethiopia
fecan
Ethiopia
linea equinocal
Nubie
y laulens
esla desoubierta portugal

Chapter VII
Geography

Why do we feel attracted to, or drawn to, certain parts of the world where we have never been, and conversely feel disinclined to visit certain countries or other parts of the world?

In meditation, or regression, these feelings have been frequently borne out by experiences registered in the Akashic records, or in our own subconscious mind from previous incarnations.

This is a good subject for meditation. It is fascinating to read books on various countries, to study and to touch art objects from different historical periods, and to meditate on them. We may in this manner wish to evoke the past to substantiate what at first may have seemed just inexplicable nostalgic feelings, or on the other hand unexplainable and seemingly unreasonable paranoic fears about certain localities or regions.

My interest in most countires lies in the coast lines, and that area extending some 50 miles inland from the coast. The only exceptions seem to be Paris and Peru. In California, this includes the Missions and the one inland exception is Monument Valley. There must be something magic about that 50-mile limit. History relates that Pompey was given control of a 50-mile strip along the coast of the Mediterranean for fiscal and military purposes. I still don't know where I got the 50-mile idea, not having found out about Pompey's doings until the present time.

I feel interested in Mexico only south of Lake Chapala, but my reaction to this land of the Aztecs is one of subconscious apprehension. On the othr hand, the Yucatan Peninsula, land of the Mayas from ancient times, has attracted me since I was 3-4 years old! The names of Uxmal, Palenque and Chichen Itza seemed familiar to me even at that early age, and awaken a resonance in my mind even now. I know I must follow this call some day. I do feel attracted to Costa Rica, but the rest of Central and South America leaves me cold, with perhaps the exception of Peru which belonged to Lemuria at one time.

On the east coast of the continent in Brazil I feel an affinity for Bahia (Salvador). I may have emigrated to these parts from Portugal in October 1497.

I had an incarnation in Portugal in the 15th century, and lived at Vila do Infante in the area of Sagres, near Cabo Sao Vicente, the south-west corner of Europe, high above the Atlantic.* However, some California friends in this life time remember visiting me in Castle Pena, near Lisbon, where I was imprisoned, they say, in that incarnation. I visited Castle Pena in this life time; my reaction was one of intense interest, as indeed — amongst my earliest drawings made as soon as I could hold a pencil were pictures of Castle Pena. The feelings that sifted through to this life, were not feelings of resentment at having been imprisoned, but rather feelings of the beauty of the place — the towers and battlements of Castle Pena with the vastness of the Atlantic Ocean as a dramatic background.

In Asia, it would be Japan — south of Tokyo only, and China — Shantung, Kiang-Su and the south coast, but only as far as the Pearl River.

The next 2 magnets are Angkor Vat and Bangkok, in Cambodia and Thailand. Interesting to me is the Temple of Borobodoer on the Island Of Java, and the Island of Bali east of Java, and some other places in this part of the globe: Kalimantan, Maluku, the Spice Islands from Ternate down to Banda of the bloody Nutmeg Wars ... beyond that the Arafura Sea holds for me fear of a shipwreck and transition.**

---

*See Voyage to Gondwana pages 74 and 75.
**See Voyage to Gondwana pages 79 to 87.

For much vaunted India I have a decided aversion, and no interest, with the exception of a territory which I was just trying to define when I happened to come across it perfectly outlined as the old Mogul Empire, not at its summit, but around 1775. I found this in the "World Book" Atlas, almost perfectly circumscribing the territory which at one time must have meant "my country" to me. It reached from just south of Agra to well north of Srinagar.

Europe and the Mediterranean area are the cradle of our western civilization, which makes it naturally interesting to many, as it is to me! I have touched upon some of my most personally magnetic spots in the Mediterranean in the chapter VOYAGES. I love Venice and the Lake Region, but am repelled by Rome and Naples, indifferent to Florence and Pisa, Genoa and Milano. I love nearby Lake Como resorts from Roman times. I shall have to research my deep attachment to Ravenna — perhaps I helped to make some of the mosaics there. I made a pilgrimmage there in 1969.

Continuing on our journey through geographical space, we should not forget the other dimension: TIME. You will find it doubly rewarding to get a good HISTORICAL ATLAS. There are some excellent ones, such as The Times of London Atlas of World History — by far the best, and The Anchor Atlas of World History by Doubleday, which gives an amazing miniature portrait of human civilization from the Stone Age on. Also, The NATIONAL GEOGRAPHIC makes it all come alive.

In this age of computer science we now have another road into personal geography opened to us. It is Astro*Carto*Graphy, which shows the relation of our personality to various parts of the world on the basis of our natal charts. I was sceptical about this newly updated science, but curious enough to find out more, so I sent for a map of the world with my natal chart superimposed on it on the basis of my birth hour.

The map and report arrived. I noticed immediately something was wrong. It did not at all agree with my personal reactions to, and experiences in, various parts of this country as well as Europe. This was frustrating to me and I was about to denounce the system when I noticed I had sent in the wrong hour of birth! I had stated 8:45 PM instead of 8:15 PM. So I sent for another chart.

The second chart was strikingly RIGHT. Everything fell into place, like a jigsaw puzzle. The difference of just 30 minutes made a whale of a difference in the calculations. This proved to me this new science was on the right track! Such a chart opens up new avenues of geographical and astrological perspectives.

A sensitive reader of Noble Prize winner Johannes V.Jensen's book, THE LONG JOURNEY, will distinctly feel how the axis of the spinning top called Earth is wobbling around its poles and how the earth's crust is slithering over its hard core in an extremely slowly continuing continental drift, as it is causing several ice ages. If you will read this, you will very likely sense the idea of reincarnation of individuals, as well as of whole groups, tribes, and even whole cultures, inspiring to recalls of former lives.

Travelers may become aware of the fact that cities also have personalities. Each has its own atmosphere. Some people will be attracted to it and others repelled. Each such community has its life-cycle,its life-span; it waxes and wanes. Being born during an upbeat era of a city will perhaps have a corresponding effect on the human being! There might be a parallel here to the astrogeographical locations on which the people of ASTRO-CARTOGRAPHY have done excellent work, determining which latitude and longitude seems to be most suitable for a person born at certain hours and in certain places — but there are probably also other factors such as the races and religions which have been prevalent in the development of such cities, and have left invisible yet indelible marks on that location. In addition to the general astronomical location, there are other more locally detailed factors involved, such as micro-climates, not commonly considered.

Hand in hand with Reincarnation and Geography goes Reincarnation and Food.

REINCARNATION AND FOOD

There seems to be some indication that food preferences may be carried over from one incarnation to another. This has occurred to me as being the answer for one person "taking to" foods never accustomed to all during early life, during the growing years. It is usually the foods one grows up with that one will want and continue to prefer over new foods. Citizens will stick to their national foods:

The Germans came over to America with their Sauerbraten and Potato Pancakes, which became naturalized in U.S.A. as "beef a la mode." They brought their deep dish Appelkuchen mit Schlagsahne and Sausages with Sauerkraut which became naturalized over here as apple pie a' la mode and frankfurters with (or without) Kraut.

The English, like their roast beef and Yorkshire pudding, and their trifle, and you will find these dishes wherever you find Englishmen. Will these eating habits carry forward into future incarnations?

I am thinking of a person who grew up in a family whose English parents enjoyed their roast beef and Yorkshire pudding. But she veered away from these foods in later years and displayed a pronounced liking for Near East, or Middle East foods like sesame seeds, dates, figs, although she certainly never saw a sesame seed, or millet, in her early life, and was unaccustomed to much citrus fruit which became a favorite. This person also veered away from many of the staple foods eaten during the first quarter-century of life, including oatmeal, meat, most cooked vegetables, puddings, corn flakes, cakes every day, and even ice-cream.

My preference is for apples, prunes, pears, lingonberries, Alpine strawberries and all other berries of northern Europe, hazel nuts, potatoes, smoked fish and pickled herring; these are all foods I grew up with. I am indifferent to fruit of the moderate zones, peaches, apricots, almonds. My genetic stock of the northern half of the northern hemisphere corresponds to my likes and dislikes. Tropical fruit does not appeal too much to me, papayas, mangos, citrus, or even bananas. I am not aware of any southern incarnations that might have become moderating factors.

Interestingly, my elder daughter tells me that although she was used to all kinds of fruit when she was growing up here in California, she really does prefer fish and vegetables! Seems to be some genetic influence here on the paternal side.

Personally, I should not have found my liking for French foods surprising, as I grew up on Hugenot food in Western Germany, so it was no change really. In any case, French food is so generally popular that it could hardly be counted even as cicumstantial evidence if somebody likes it!

On the other hand, I took to Russian food, also, as soon as I got acquanted with it, which may be a point for my thesis, but hardly any proof. My favorite Russian food is fish stew, Ribnaya Selianka, and I think that Russian pastries are simply wonderful. Another favorite Russian food is Sirniki, a pancake on a basis of "baker's cheese." Bortsch is another choice and these 3 Russian foods are my very favorite foods. I do feel this argues in favor of my having had a Russian life.

Almost a stronger argument in favor of favorite flavors being passed along from incarnation to incarnation is my experience with Chinese food of which I am very fond. I did not have to "get used to" that. When I first was introduced to Chinese food at the International House at the University in New York, my Chinese friend just showed me once how to handle the chopsticks, and to his amazement I fell right to without any difficulty. I can still pick up even a single grain of rice without any difficulty. I definitely did not find that anything NEW to learn. My fingers got the instruction directly from the subconscious; I feel sure I must have used chopsticks probably in the 14th and 15th Centuries, all the way down from Shantung to Annam. I distinctly prefer the quick-cooked Oriental foods in general. As a native of Shantung,

I prefer Mandarin or other northern Chinese cooking.

I also love the very spicy foods of Szechuan. I must have had some of that "at home." Perhaps my mother came from that "far west."

On the other hand, the hot and spicy foods of Mexico leave me cold, whereas I do like the foods of Spain.

One type of food which I certainly never tasted during the first 30 years of my current life was a group of Mediterranean fish soups and fish stews, such as bouillabaisse, Spanish seafood combinations, Illyrian and Greek fish dishes. To all these I took to instantly, and they are still favorites of mine even though I suspect I was fed some of them on an Algerian galley in the 16th century. (From which I still retain occasional feelings of oppressive claustrophobia.)

While foods often seem to reflect ancient customs from the geographical areas of other lives, the same may be said about clothing. I have a friend who had nothing whatsoever of Russian influence in her ancestry but who likes to have her head tied up in a Babushka, commonly worn by women in Russia rural area, but which none of her Russian acquaintances in America do. She also makes clothes for herself that are medieval in character or design. Her dress may be made of colored squares of several different colors, like old divisions of coats-of-arms.

Another entire group of peculiar clothing habits is that of the hippies, so prevalent in the last few decades. Many of them dress as much like American Indians as they can, going as far as to put one feather in their headbands! I am convinced this is a hangover from previous lives, and that many of them were reborn after living as American Indians in the previous century, and now exhibiting protest or hostility against the "establishment" that they were born into in their present lives. They are acting in protest out of resentment welling up from their subconscious against the white people who mistreated them.

Food customs seem to persist through generations and recipes are handed down from mother to daughter, and from great, great grandmother to great, great granddaughter!

I found this confirmed in a most unexpected quarter when I was spending a weekend relaxing between business appointments in Loudun in the Loire Valley in France, when I got into a conversation with a man of about 50 years of age. We talked about the wars between France and Germany, and he told me he had been a POW in Germany during WWI. I presumed this had been quite a hard time for him but no — it was a very good time, for while everybody else was getting shot at he was simply doing farm work as he did at home, and the food was almost the same. Even the girls wore the same headdresses — the white coiffes of the Bretagne — so he felt quite at home. This made it obvious to me that he had been in Hessen, where all the best recipes had been introduced by the French Hugenots that found refuge in Germany after Louis XIV abolished freedom of religion in France in 1685, driving some 300,000 people into exile. So to this day the sausages of Hessen are the equal of the best to be found at the annual Foire de Paris (Fair), where the best produce of the country is brought.

When in Germany, I talked to quite a few Hugenot farmers. Most of them have completely lost their awareness of their French descent and do not understand a word of French, but feel as German Nationals. However, their names are still French, and the proverbs over the doors of their half-timbered houses common to the area are in French, moreover the recipes and festival costumes have been handed down for 8 generations. Their famous "bacon cake" is still brought out at festival time, it is one of their customs. I shall always remember when I tasted it for the first time (in this life!). It was a feast for my tastebuds, but it was more — it was tied up with a nostalgia of bygone lives.

Chapter VIII
Reincarnation and Architecture

From their earliest beginnings, places of worship were built to appeal to people's feelings and emotions, and thus to make deep impressions on their subconscious minds.

Early structures, such as the temples of Greece and Magna Graecia made an almost purely mental appeal through the harmonious simplicity of their mathematical proportions of their straight lines, obviously derived from Egypt.

This I experienced personally in Poseidonia in the South of Naples in Italy, and in Akragas, Sicily. As a child I had been surrounded in my father's study by a number of pictures of Greek temples and Greek statuary. I had always felt his reverence for Greek art was a bit excessive, and even at my first sight of the temples I still felt that way. However, as a painter I could not resist the temptation to sit down on the Sicilian hillside and draw a few temples. As I was drawing, I felt the understanding of my father's feelings now enter my head through my hands. I felt I had walked here before.

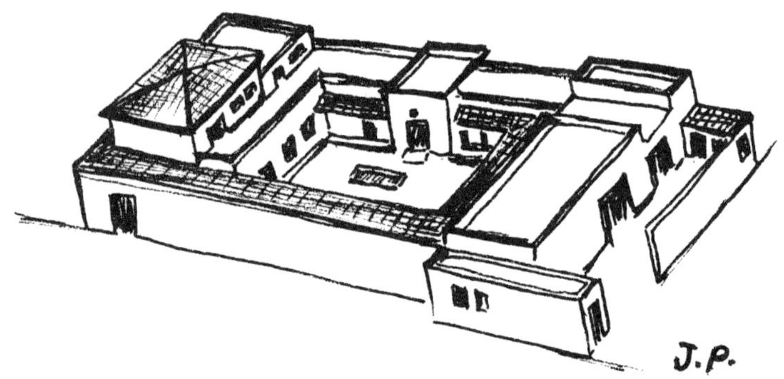

If you should wander into a certain antique type of residence with the living quarters built around a central atrium or court, you may feel stirred in your depths as having lived in such a dwelling in a past life. This was the principal design for dwellings for thousands of years, familiar to us chiefly through Greek and Roman architecture, and through the Chinese "courts." They are simply a number of atrium-centered units attached to the original unit.

We can still see them in some types of buildings here in California, and in large numbers in Mexico. They are good places to meditate on the past. Try it during a quiet siesta period. It may take you back 2000 years or more.

Romance style churches formed the first step toward a more emotional appeal, with their softer, rounder lines. I must say I did not experience this in the earlier plain stone specimens, but with the mosaic-adorned cathedrals of Sicily, Ravenna and Venice, I became fully aware of their spiritual impact, and they stirred memories of past lives.

St. Peter's in Rome, on the other hand, impressed me as an oriental orgy of sensuality, almost repulsive! In self-defense, I may state I have heard other people voice this same reaction after a visit to this supposedly supreme Christian shrine.

The large Bavarian and Franconian Abbey churches seem overpowering and overly decorated with their painted ceilings. They seem to have inherited some of their style from St. Peter's. They evoked no warm feelings in me.

How different were the Gothic Cathedrals of Europe! Their Rose Windows automatically induced space flights during the centuries before the invention of transcendental meditation. I have visited a lot of churches and cathedrals, but was most impressed with Chartres, Notre Dame de Paris, Cologne and Munich.

If one can forget the gingerbread outside — and I managed to do so — one might find the most impressive of all to be the interior of the Duomo of Milan. There the heat from hundreds of burning votive candles and tapers wafts one's spirit along and up in an incense-flavored cloud of warm air, up and up along the vertical runways of the ultimate outer darkness of the top reaches of the nave. One does not need much imagination here to visualize the bodily assumption of Mary from this starting pad, perhaps with the prophet Ezekiel as her space pilot. (Ezekiel 1)

Another type of building which affects my subconscious very strongly is the "German Renaissance" type of house. They are totally different from the more familiar Renaissance of Souther Europe. They are high-gabled structures adapted to the heavy snow loads of Northern Europe. Their "stepped gables" are found chiefly in Northern Germany and other "Low" countries, which until the middle of the 17th century were still part of Germany. The architects in those days moved freely about. As an example, Dutch architects built some of their finest buildings, their masterpieces, in Cologne, and farther inland. These "stepped gables" for some reason thrill me deeply, whether they are in Bremen, Brugge, or any of the Hanseatic cities. Could I have been a bricklayer — they are practically all brick structures — some stone ornaments — but I think I did not just do the work, my association seems to have to do with more basic, structural design.

There are the half-timbered dwellings of North Western Europe, that may give you as they do me a warm, homelike feeling. They are found in the lowlands of Europe from England and Normandy through Northern Germany to Southern Scandinavia.

Another category of structures that has some strange attraction for me are the Spanish Missions of California. I have felt a compulsion to visit the Missions, have seen all those in Alta California and I hope to visit those in Baja California. I referred to them in my poem, "Which Church?" I used to be very puzzled about why I made these pilgrimages, but have come to feel strongly that I was a Franciscan Padre in a previous life. At times, my spouse has "noticed" this monk personality, and has called me a "poet-monk," along with a good friend of ours who exhibits the same studious personality of a monk. We are both Franciscans in spirit, and Latin has remained our favorite vehicle for spiritual communication.

Other art forms have probably come down through genetic channels or incarnations. Closely connected with architecture are inscriptions on monuments and public buildings.

I have a very strong feeling about CAPITAL letters, a feeling of being prejudiced in favor of capitals. The feeling seems to come out of my subconscious, from centuries of familiarity with inscriptions in CAPs only. When I heard about some endeavors in various European countries to abolish capitals altogether, I felt they were letting the languages down.

Classical LATIN was WRITTEN IN CAPITALS — only. A habit derived most probably from the original inscriptions on monuments, temples, houses, or tombstones, where all the letters had to be chiseled into the marble or sandstone, which would have made "lower case" letters impractical and illegible.

Even the cuneiform letters don't seem to have disappeared entirely from the subconscious of Western people. Were they handed down through the genes of the Assyrians through the Hittities to Hessia? One correspondent of mine has a handwriting I find hard to explain (and to read): it reminds me of cuneiform script. Another correspondent has an elegant handwriting, regular and almost beautiful, but hard to read and it's like trying to read Sanscrit.

The architecture of Islam leaves a deep impression on me every time I enter a Mosque, as I often did in Paris. It is, I believe, the complete absence of "graven images," which leads me into almost instant meditation, there being NO distraction by any THING.

It is strange how Christian places of worship have lost this valuable quality by publicly flaunting their constant and massive breaking the prohibition of representational art in their sanctums. Strange that only Muslims and Jews seem to keep their commandment, proclaimed in the Book sacred to all 3 faiths. At the time of the Reformation, the iconoclasts whitewashed the walls of many a Catholic church, but after a while (up to 3 centuries that is) the old pictures were restored and the commandment forgotten, if it was ever obeyed.

Another style of the architect's drawing pen which never fails to invite my subconscious to a flight to the stars is the transcendental upswing of the lower ends of the winged Chinese roofs. I first experienced their magic in Chinese-influenced Portugal where the first European explorers of China (and Japan) had "brought back" with them this tyle, with which they were obviously as fascinated as I was. They even have the motive recurring in a small way in their — dove-cotes — decorative chimneys.*

Look, think and meditate, and you will find some structures that will seem meaningful to you, and that you may be able to use as launching pads for flights into the Past.

Chapter IX
Battle Cries

A Battle Cry, or War Cry, is defined as a cry, whether a shout or a significant name or phrase, uttered by a body of fighters to encourage each other in charging the enemy or in rallying to the fray.

If you are a Frenchman, the *Marseillaise* will make your heart beat faster, as will the mention of Lord Nelson for an Englishman, and the *Star Spangled Banner* for an American, who will also get a lift from hearing the names of General MacArthur or General Patton. The Hurray! or the Hip, Hip, Hurrah! of England or Germany has never stirred me, nor has tracing its origin back to the Hittite: Shnurri, or Hurri, from Asia Minor, ignored by modern dictionaries.

On the other hand, the words "Vlaanderen en de Leeuw" have some profound effect on me through some recesses of my subconscious that I have not yet been able to fathom. It is, of course, associated with the rampant lion in the Coat-of-Arms of Flanders. My pronounced liking for this heraldic animal has hurt my relations with the opposite political party, but was too strong to deny. I have feelings of admiration for the Artevelde family, although I was more closely associated with Jan van Artevelde than with his more famous brother Jakob van Artevelde, the Lion of Flanders, who was the Public Tribune and Captain General of the Flemish cities.

Have you ever felt that some ancient motto or device (or devise) from some king's or some country's coat-of-arms reverberated in your heart to a point where your feelings seemed to take over from reason and you did not understand the cause?

There have been such "magic" words since the beginning of history, and even before. The chief or medicine man needed warriors ready to fight for bigger and "better" causes than a rabbit or a deer, or their own cabbage patch.

What were the ancient battle cries that brought the conquering armies of the Antique to the ferocious pitch of excitement so that, unquestioning, they would eagerly rush to "do or die"?

The cleverest approach for such early day demagogues probably was to plainly break several Commandments, simultaneously using the name of God irreverently, swearing to one falsehood, or several, and inciting their men to covet their neighbor's positions, property and wives, and for good measure making them worship idols of gold or silver.

The first Crusade was largely built on "God wills it!" (from the original French: "Dieu le veut!") There were other famous battle cries: "Montjoie St. Denys!" and "Dieu et mon droit!" (God and my right!)

Today's battle cry: "We shall overcome!" has been used by different groups. It is very effective and has almost reached the level of the oldest cries! The old, original battle cry of the Muslims: "Allah Akbar!" (God is great!) has not lost a whit of its old effectiveness after 1300 years of use.

A battle cry is a slogan, stemming from the word "slughahairm" meaning host-cry employed by Scottish Highlanders or native Irish, usually consisting of a personal surname or the name of a gathering place.

Wave writes of the battle at Val-es-Dunes in 1047:

"De la gent donc esteit emmie

Poinst li cheval criant "Tur aie." ("Tur aid!" = "Thor help!")

(Thor, the old war-god of the Northmen.)

What was probably one of the most usual war-cries of the pagan Vikings still seems to have been used in moments of stress by their slightly Christianized descendants. The Vikings who raided Europe from Iceland to the White Sea, and from Portugal to Constantinople, Volga to the Caspian and Black Seas, were known as "Thor's hammer," after their thunderbolt casting war-god.

The Saxons at Senlac shouted "Holy Cross!" and "God Almighty!" but as the fight grew hotter they simply cried "Out! Out!"

In the Battle of Naseby, Prince Rupert at the head of his Cavaliers, in white sash and plume, flamed in brilliant gallantry over the field shouting, "Queen Mary! Queen Mary!" One wonders what there could be in such a cry to incite the soldiers to furious fighting. In any case, he lost the battle.

The war-cry, "crie de guerre" of the French, is of the remotest antiquity; likewise that of the Scotch, but the battle-cry of the Israelites: "The sword of the Lord and of Gideon!" (used when the Israelites engaged the hosts of Midian in the Valley of Jezreel) is perhaps the earliest record of the use of the war-cry which, now little used among civilized nations, still finds its representation in the war-whoop of the savage.

Each nation usually invoked its patron saint. So widely did the practice prevail in England, that in 1495 an Act of Parliament was passed forbidding all these cries as productive of discord, and enjoining all noblemen and their retainers thenceforth to call only on "St. George and the King!" Shakespeare gives it as the cry of each chief at the Battle of Bosworth Field:
"Sound, drums and trumpets, boldly and cheerfully,
God and St. George! Richmond and victory!"
Prince Edward exclaims, before Tewkesbury's fatal fight:
"Then strike up, drums! God and St. George for us!"
The old ballad runs:
"St. George, he was for England,
St. Denys was for France;
Sing, Honi soit qui mal y pense!"
The cry of Scotland was: "St. Andrew!"
Do any old Battle Songs stir up inexplicable emotions? — *"Over there!"* — *"Marching Through Georgia!"* — *"Mandalay!"* — *"La Marseillaise!"* — *"La Giovinezza!"* — *"Tipperary!"* — *"Fahne Hoch!"* — *"Rule, Britannia!"* — *"Sailing Against Engelland!"*

Battle cries, or Slogans, have not figured in my vocabulary, but I had one experience when I created a new one myself on the spur of the moment. It was, however, not born out of enthusiasm but rather repartee, and served the purpose beautifully at the moment.

It was in the fall before Pearl Harbor. I was in Hamburg, Germany, to handle the transfer of some business to some Italian friends to prevent its being confiscated at the impending entry of the USA into World War II. I had just stepped into an elevator in a business building in which there was already a passenger.

He stretched out his arm in a $45°$ angle in a very aggressive Nazi salute and shouted: "Heil Hitler!" Maybe he thought I was a Jew! Anyway, I reacted automatically and instantly with an equally vigorous "HEIL ROOSEVELT!" It was a pleasure to see his jaw drop down, and I was very pleased with myself although I had never at any time been an admirer of Franklin D. Roosevelt.

The gesture of the Nazi salute, with an open palm and the arm extended at a $45°$ angle, seems much more aggressive than the Communist salute of defiance with the extended closed fist. The Nazi salute had a subconscious hypnotizing effect on both the giver and the recipient who was supposed to answer immediately and emphatically under penalty of Ostracism. On me it had the opposite effect — it raised my adrenal reaction to the point where I was inspired to shout out instantly a very effective squashing reply, without having had time to think about it. Under slightly different circumstances it might have landed me in a Concentration Camp (no, I am not a Jew). The "Heil Hitler!" slogan must be counted as one of the most electrifying slogans of all times. It is difficult to realize that unless one has witnessed its application even in small groups, not to mention the national Party Day meetings, that we have seen and heard on TV.

Even stronger than any of the Battle Cries of the Western World — perhaps the strongest of all — was the Muslims' "Allah Akbar!" ("God is great!"). This stirred the followers of the Prophet to a burning heat of enthusiasm and carried the banners of their small armies of a few thousand from Arabia to the Atlantic within a century, and later as far as Central Asia, ultimately into South-East Asia.

Officially, starting with the Hegira ("migration," not "flight") in 622, it reached its first peak within 144 years at the time of the birth of Harun Al Rashid.

We can turn our back on any slogan consciously, but slogans that have been repeated over and over may not sway us but may have an unacknowledged effect on our subconscious mind.

This is what happens in the world of advertising — some of which is very powerful.

Slogans today have become so vulgarized by Madison Avenue that they have become trite cliches,but there are still a few of the old ones that carry weight today, even deprived of their mediaeval punch and glamor.

Chapter X
Whence — Our Two Souls?

"Two souls, alas! are fighting in my breast." Thus said Goethe, the poet. Maybe the explanation is that if we are the product of many long experiences through reincarnation we are also shaped by a probably more physical inheritance handed down to us through the bloodlines. It seems necessary to take this into account to understand the working of reincarnation, which in turn explains "What is thicker than blood?"

On the world stage, it seems it was Sir Walter Scott who first used the expression: "Bluid is thicker than water" though it probably goes bcak to a much older proverb. It has been repeated often since and is commonly used in reference to the Atlantic Ocean between Britain and the United States.

However, there must be something even deeper than blood in our makeup, our Atma, or Ka, or Personality, or whatever name you may wish to give to the entity that carries forward certain qualities and abilities or feelings from one incarnation to the following ones. Where are the roots of age-old sympathies or antipathies lodged? Is language thicker than blood? It certainly is the vehicle for the expression of a people's innermost feelings. We have all seen apparent feelings — difficult to explain — displayed by others. Where did they come from?

I am a puzzle to myself. I am a direct lineal descendant of Henry "The Lion," ruler of Saxony and Bavaria.' I cannot deny a certain amount of appreciation for his sometimes effective tactics. However, I was deeply opposed to his over all strategies, and have carried that feeling down to even his other descendants, the entire Welf family.

Theoretically, if you go by bloodlines, you would call me a Welf, but in practice I have always been on the side of the Ghibellines, and against the Guelphs, as they called them in Italy through the centuries.

Yes, you may object: "That is a typical sour grapes story. You are descended through the morganatic wife of Henry, The Lion, which must have given you an inferiority complex." I understand your doubts, but Duke Henry was always well regarded by her family. He treated her as well as could be expected, endowing her richly with properties in Westphalia. Part of these lands, the "DEIKEN AKERS" or Deikenfeld, were handed down for over 700 years in the Decken family. On May 16, 1891 there were 44 heirs shown as participants in the old Feudal Lien in the county books. The County Real Estate records show both the old family name as Deicke and the modern version of Decken. The last piece of these estates was apparently sold by my grandfather's father, Christian Heinrich (Thunderstorm) Decken, who according to all accounts seemed to have inherited some of the less desirable characteristics of the famous ancestor, and in fact passed some of them along down the line.

One could hardly have expected Henry to divorce his official second wife, Princess Matilda, whom he probably married for political reasons. This daughter of Henry II, King of England, saved more than his life when he found shelter at her father's court, the Plantagenet Court. There were, however, never any ill feelings voiced against the "Lion" in our family.

Yet, many years later, I found myself still in the camp that opposed the Welfs: the Ghibellines and the imperial family at the Court of Frederick II, that Norman Emperor of the "Roman Empire of the German Nation," whom I served as District Attorney in Palermo, Sicily, his capital.

The Welf party finally won when the Pope reaped the harvest of the Hohenstaufen's catastrophic collapse at Tagliacozzo. By then I had already left Sicily for France and my interest in the affairs of Italy and Germany ended.

From that time on, all their later rulers left me completely cold and uninterested. But having espoused the cause of the Ghibelline Hohenstaufen and d'Hauteville families was a strange thing to do—for a Welf. Trying to transpose this to an American frame of reference: it might be likened to a Boston descendent of the Pilgrims becoming a standard-bearer of Jefferson Davis, the President of the Confederacy.

Anyway, two traditions are fighting in my mind. Do others feel like I do? Streams of the subconscious run deep. Only once in a while do they seem to well up to the surface of consciousness. Where is the source of my constant sympathy for the underdog? My physical blood lines run along the chain of top dogs, from Henry, The Lion, and others through many generations of bishops, supreme court justices, university principals and deans, senators and councilmen. Yet a native Welf was an enthusiastic Ghibelline, until they became the underdogs, when my interest ceased, surprisingly, or because of the end of the D'Hautevilles?

As a person without any Western Hemisphere incarnation, how could I have always had a strong sympathy for the South?

Whence, my general sympathy for the underdog? A love of liberty? My spiritual ancestors certainly were of a different brand, always independent thinkers, worshippers of Aton and Mithra, Essenes, Arian heretics, Gnostics, Albigensians, Waldensians, Hugenots, Protestants. Here, however, the blood lines converge. I had two Hugenot grandmothers! Are they still fighting my establishment grandfathers inside me?

The apparent struggle between two frequently contrasting basic causes is the polarity between genes and "BOMs" — Biological Organizing Model. I have adopted this expression from Guy Playfair (who wrote "The Infinite Boundary") and Hernani G. Andrade, the Brazilian scientist.

BOM is one of the facets of the entity of Monad — the metaphysical transmitter of characteristics or thoughts from previous entity or entities, equivalent to the genes which are transmitters on the physical level.

I have a theory on split personalities. Maybe there is a physical basis to this cliche. Maybe there are actually bloodlines fighting in my veins, or at least in tragical split personalities. What is going on in the seemingly changing personalities of so many international figures, so idealistic and yet destructive in their final effects on humanity?

As Freeman Dyson, the atom scientist, said: "Nothing is so dangerous as an idealist!" To which I would like to add: "especially in regard to elected political leaders," or self-annointed saviors of humanity, such as Jim Jones, Dr. Moon, or organizers of other cults, such as Children of God.

Chapter XI
Transvital Recycling

The more I think about the "LAST judgement" the more I come to the conclusion that this expression is to be taken literally. In other words, there must be other prior-judgments. It seems logical that such a LAST judgment should be held on the potter's field, where the divine potter would then recycle our common clay shards into silica dust, thus completing the ecological cycle of economy of the universe, according to which nothing is ever lost.

The application of this principle is quite obvious in all chemical and biochemical processes. Solids may be melted into liquids, burnt into gases, liquids evaporated and condensed again — and so we come from dust and return to dust. Energy often is created from matter and may re-enter into the creation of new matter. Nothing is annihilated.

Recycling of course involves a breaking down into basic components. Usually this is done through the application of heat, melting in the "crucible," so often mentioned symbolically in philosophical and alchemical literature. Maybe we should take this expression, "the crucible," literally too. Any not otherwise usable substances will be reduced to new dust in the "fire of hell."

Where is hell? People have always asked that. Poseidonios of Rhodos was perhaps the first who came out openly in saying that it cannot be in the earth, as the earth is solid — nor at the antipodes.

It is interesting to note that the old Scandinavians pictured hell as a place where it would be "cold as hell," since it was inconceivable for them that warmth could be excessive.

On the other hand, the general idea of southern people was that it was "hot as hell," as they liked the cool part of the year in their moderate climates. In fact, the Greeks, with their ideal Mediterranean climate, even included the ideal "Elysian fields" in their idea of the underworld.

The "fire of hell" of the New Testament was the "Gehenna," the eternally burning fires on the dumping grounds of the city of Jerusalem, where much of the garbage was incinerated for hygienic reasons. There was, of course, no recycling, but just breaking down into "dust." Here was a good demonstration of the words: "from dust to dust."

Nor is this a new, or even recent, theory: the Greeks have an almost identical story: "Man springs from the soot from the burning bodies of the Titans that Zeus slew after they had murdered and eaten his son Zangreus, whose mother was Persephone, the Earth. Hence, man has now in him a small divine element from Zangreus and a large wicked element from the Titans, and has to perfect himself slowly in many incarnations before he can be accepted as a hero on Mount Olympus.

Hence, as G.L. Playfair puts it: "The whole history of man has been that of his dual behavior, the conflict between intelligence and bestial behavior."

About the year 1000 B.C. the Rig-Veda stated: "The souls of the righteous at death would travel to the world of the fathers, where they would enjoy the fruit of their right living. Then they would return to earth and there become food, consumed by man, then pass into the womb of woman to be reborn into new bodies. But the souls of those who lives evil lives would be reborn as animals, or even as insects."

The theory that death is the end of the personality is a recent one, and exclusively of Western man.

Not only the Egyptians, but even the Neanderthals, provided their dead with supplies for their next life, such as food, tools, pets, servants and wives which were sometimes just wooden models, sometimes actual people.

TRANSMIGRATION

In general, the word "transmigration" refers to the changeover when a soul is reborn in a new and different body. In the more limited and pejorative sense of the word, this refers to the possible re-embodiment of a human soul in an animal body. This is considered a real possibility in the East, but a pagan "superstition" in the West.

However, Saint Justin, the martyr, explains that the soul of man occupies a human body on more than one occasion. He even thinks that maybe the souls of the worst sinners might be reborn in wild or tame animals! Such beliefs are supposed to be held only by what is called the "less informed in many Asian countries." It seems to me that certain "human" beings are so inhuman that they might do very well with an incarnation in an animal body. This might teach them a lot about human fiends …

Aside from the transmigration of human souls into animals, which is looked upon with disfavor by most writers, it seems they also deny collective souls for dogs or horses, or cats. Maybe so, but it may be wishful thinking of those humans who also deny specific reincarnation for single animals. One of the greatest of all philosophers, Pythagoras, did not apparently think so. However, he had hardly passed away when one of his pupils, under the weight of public opinion, had to apologize for him.

"Anima" means "soul," so apparently early and less conceited human beings felt that animals did have animas. Some affirm that animals do not suffer as we humans do. One wonders what basis there is for such an idea when there is visual evidence to the contrary, as owners of hundreds of thousands of pets will testify. Considering dogs the spiritual descendants of wolves, and cats of lions or tigers, was there not karmic improvement of their soul personalities when they came out of the woods to become companions and helpmates to mankind?

Transmigration of human souls into animal bodies was a taboo subject even amongst liberal philosophers. It hurts their egos and would probably drive away possible pious converts. Would animals be better treated if human beings thought they had souls? Probably not, judging from the way human (not humane) beings treat each other. In addition to the objection to restriction in choices for our future lives, I find the majority of scholars rebelling eo ipso against the possibility of transmigration, yet Pythagoras did not cast it aside. Could it be that he was right and the others wrong? Was it that they were afraid that a shocked and humiliated public might castigate them and that the "in" people of the time might even have them burnt at the stake? We know that people were sentenced to death, by church or state, for lesser "machinations of the devil," such as doubting the geocentric nature of the universe.

Or was it that the pillars of church and society were shocked at the thought that they themselves might be subject to such a law if they admitted its existence, and so preferred to stick their heads into the sand rather than to experience the deep personal humiliation that deep inside they subcconsciously felt they needed to make up misdeeds?

Even numerous Eastern thinkers and groups have negated or put aside the thought of transmigration. Often it surely was to avoid the scorn of Western philosophers. One might say they swept this taboo tradition under the carpet, at least when Western "visitors were expected."

Most Christian thinkers, at least in public, and with just 2-3 exceptions, have always been very uptight upon this subject. They seem to have found it the most effective weapon against this disagreeable controversial subject to ignore it completely and bury it in deep silence, so it would not be brought to the attention of the general public.

This attitude was, and still is, so generally prevalent that it seems to me that "The lady" (publicly expressed opinion of teachers) "protesteth too much," as they are afraid that if the possibility of transmigration was even discussed it might detract from their dignity in front of their students. They are afraid that even lifting the hem of their purple mantle of power might hurt their "honors" (in old Roman times this was equivalent to "honoraries"). Of course they do not have a clear conscience and therefore are scared, afraid that others might see them as their subconscious, or THE LAW, might judge them, even if the law would not.

In modern times, consistent with coming of the Age of Aquarius, secret teachings and hidden knowledge is being brought to the surface everywhere. Light is being shed into the deep recesses; caves of superstition and sacred cows are being reduced to their natural functions and destinies. Taboos are being broken everywhere, so it seems appropriate time for at least an open discussion and examination of the age-old Eastern Doctrine of Transmigration.

Many teachers nowadays are courageous enough, when they have a clear conscience, not to be afraid that their students will honor them less if they admit that we are ALL subject to the LAW OF CAUSE AND EFFECT.

There is probably no way at our present stage of research into matters metaphysical to prove or to disprove the possibility of transmigration. However, it seems that if a healthy fear of the possibility of its existence would be injected into some people they might think twice about shameful behavior, that if they behaved worse (?) than animals they might be reborn and treated as such. Such a healthy fear might help to keep many on a straight and narrow path, though it would not eliminate ALL crime as many people would not care about the consequences, still not understanding the law of cause and effect. Right now what makes people reject the doctrine of transmigration, like many other thoughts from Eastern wisdom, is the fear of humiliation.

Some philosophers, who were trying to reconcile the "animal" story with their presumptive beliefs, stated that the animals mentioned would simply be the names of the constellations of the zodiac, such as the ram, the bull, and the lion, that the souls would have to transmigrate through. This counter-clockwise progression around the zodiac sounded a lot more acceptable to the thinkers who were willing to admit that they might need some punishment for their deeds, but whose dignity was hurt by thinking that they might be condemned to get it in animal form. On the other hand, the great philosopher and mathematician, Pythagoras, apparently thought it quite natural and appropriate that an imperfect human might be put through a course in a "correctional facility" inside the body of an animal.

If some writers consider transmigration to be a retrogressive system, this does not seem well-founded. Spirals or waves may all go up and down without excluding the over-all progressive direction of the over-all system.

In school, students sometimes have to take a certain grade over again, going backward like planets appear to do when they are "retrograde" (apparently moving backwards), but they are actually not moving backwards but only appear to be doing so from our terrestrial point of view of observation.

In this modern age of statistics, cycles and graphs, are there any that do not go up and down? Should the cycles we are looking at here be the only exception in nature? Population and crime figures do not go upwards only, but in between have dips and summits.

What is my opinion? Well, "Ignoramus ignorabimus." ("There is much that we do not know and will not know.") I feel, as the old Italian proverb has it, "Si non e vero, e ben trovato." ("If it is not true, it is at least well invented.")

If man will be afraid of a possibility of being put into a correctional facility, such as the body of an animal, it will be at least the equivalent of our "Christian" fear of brimstone and eternal hell fire, and might be a lot more effective than capital punishment (hardly ever carried out, anyhow).

Thus, publicizing transmigration might not be a bad idea.

It is by now generally accepted that we incarnate in the male form in some lives and in the female form in some lives — although even here the "battle of sexes" enters into this belief. Some very male males object to the idea of having been a female, and a feminine-female sometimes objects to the idea of having been a male! All things considered, a little alternation now and then is recognized as being beneficial in striking a balance — keeping the males and females from being too concentrated, too dominating, too submissive.

Some human beings bear a startling resemblance to some kind of animal, or bird or creature of the sea. Have we not all encountered human beings who made us exclaim to our spouses in an aside, "Gosh, look, doesn't that man look like a goat?" There are motherly women who look like mother hens, men with horse faces, catty girls, and those with a St. Bernard look. I know a squirrelly girl, who is cute and also flits about like a squirrel and loves nuts. When I was a school boy my peers called me "fish-mouth" during a period when I was not too happy. Nowadays I grin like a cat, and also sneeze like a cat and love to lie in the sun. I can purr, too. One friend "re-members" being a water snake, not hard to believe if you saw her shape!

Consider that the human embryo goes through a number of evolutionary stages while developing in the womb, which appear to correspond to stages gradually passing from amoebae-like through fish-like and mammal-like forms.

Some of the images of the gods of most ancient people: Egypt, Sumeria, Middle America, look very weird. Some have human bodies but heads of falcon, lion, cow, ram, and dog. There was the bull-headed Minotaur in Crete and the donkey in Mid-summer Night's Dream, and the fairy tales in which people were turned into animals, and vice versa. What is one to make of all this? Some are undoubtedly just symbolic, like Odysseus' companions being turned into "pigs" by Circe when she overfed them at a feast. But is there something behind all that smoke of men being turned into animals, and animals into men, gods assuming the shape of animals, in the mythology of practically all nations, tribes?

Were there possibly, under the Mendelian Law, some throw-backs to the days the Theosophists call "The FALL of MAN"? Or are they cases of arrested fetal development? The early days of mankind were shrouded in mystery and the facts, or memory of which was only very selectively handed down in some of the earliest Mystery Schools.

CHOICE OF VEHICLE

In many of the books I have read dealing with rebirth I have found the affirmative that the entity can choose the vehicle for the next life — that is, the soul about to reincarnate can choose the race into which it will reincarnate, or the family, as well as the sex and the state of well-being, degree of culture, and opportunity for prospering. Some writers even say it will be able to choose whether or not it is to return at this time, or at all. This latter alternative seems to me to be quite presumptive and unrealistic. If there IS a law, there is order and system, and not chaos caused by the individual's foibles or fits, or wishful thinking.

Another theory, which seems to me a little more logical is: that less developed entities are being automatically assigned to generally suitable roles for the next time around, whereas more developed personalities are being directed toward contributing to the choice of vehicle for their next incarnation. At least this is what human beings would like to believe. The question of determinism or indeterminism has always been one where *feeling* more than *reasoning* has tended to influence opinions.

One thing, however, has to be said: If there is such a thing as precognition then there must be predetermination. This hurts the ego of proud humans. We want free will at any cost, even at the cost of justice and life or death, and happiness.

If there is at least a choice of vehicles, then there should be some evidence bearing it out. The nearest place to check for this seems to be one's own case, family and friends, so I'll start with mine. My personal experience seems to confirm what has been proclaimed by the reincarnation specialists.

There seem to be 2 principal strains involved: the blood lines and the reincarnation lines. Considering my great interest in linguistics and poetry, I can easily understand why I would want to be "born again" into the Endemann family with its 7 consecutive generations of Protestant parsons and bishops, through 3 centuries, forming a steady academic background, as my direct line ancestors. They were all nominally "protestant" — yet really that is a misnomer. If one looks closely at the facts, the so-called "protestants" within a short time after their ascendancy became at least as dogmatic as the old church against which they had protested! These tendencies probably were reinforced when these clerics married almost exclusively daughters of other parsons in the reformed church of Hessen. My grandfather, Johann Conrad Endemann, followed the tradition when he married his first 2 wives (2 sisters), and the offpsring of these 2 marriages confirmed the tendency, with my father's 2 oldest brothers becoming bishops.

However, there must have been somewhere in the background of Johann Conrad's soul a stirring or revival of that true protestant spirit, which urged him on toward an adventure in spiritual liberty when he married his 3rd wife! She was a pastor's daughter (it would have been too shocking if she had not been) BUT she was an almost pure-bred Hugenot, a descendant of the last really "protesting" independent thinkers. Besides this, she was almost pure Breton — and, as such, a "squarehead." The 2 sons resulting from this third marriage were the first Endemanns NOT to take the cloth, but over the strong protest from their still traditional father.

Johann Conrad wrote first 2 small volumes of spiritual poems and hymns that were published. After that he wrote wordly poems which were apocrypha — not published. They were by no means shocking but would hardly have been appropriate for a bishop.

His younger son was Georg Theobald, my father. He had 300 years of Latin and Greek, and some Aramaic and Hebrew study in his inheritance, but he would not let himself be forced to use these facilities for the pulpit where he strongly felt he would be maneuvered into hypocrisy. So he became a teacher of classical languages and physical education. He had also inherited his father's talent for writing and his mother's cheerful disposition, these came out as very fine, worldly poetry. He had 2 volumes published, in addition to many magazine and newspaper articles.

When the time came for him to get married, his choice was directed toward another Hugenot (50%), a cheerful and very fine but unorthodox girl, who was to become my mother.

With these factors in my background, no wonder I am another squarehead, although by no means a square.

SQUAREHEAD

Ma tête carrée
A quatre faces,
Franque et Saxonne,
Normande, Bretonne.

My square head has
Of faces four,
Frankish, Norman,
Saxon, Breton.

Ce qui reflète précisement
La composition de mon sang
Du côté de mère, et père:
Mes quatre arrière grandmères.

Which quite precisely
Now reflect my blood
My mother's side, my father's side,
My great-grandmothers' four.

So it seems to me that if there is a considerable freedom of choice in looking for a vehicle, it would be quite likely that my entity was bound to look for some parents like these with their old family traditions, yet free spirits and minds. I soaked up all the Greek art and Roman literature there was around our house, and my father's poetry with its lyrical, dramatic and spiritual inspiration. THIS OBVIOUSLY WAS THE AMBIANCE THAT I HAD WISHED FOR WHEN CHOOSING MY PARENTS.

Now, looking further back, the same theory seems to be confirmed. In all the incarnations of which I am conscious I have always been an independent thinker, Hugenot, rebel, heretic, protestant (when that still meant "protesting"), Cathare, Albigensian, Internationalist in Sicily, philosopher and alchemist, Rosicrucian, in the Middle Ages, and before that a Gnostic, follower of Manes, worshipper of Mithra, and worker for Akhnaton, and thus very likely the same thing before that.

However, unlike so many people nowadays (perhaps too many), I have no remembrance of Atlantis, except perhaps that there constantly reappears on the screen of my memory a huge reversed cone of a cloud towering above a conical volcano. It reminds me of the myth of Atlas carrying earth or heaven on his shoulders. Rightly or wrongly I identify it subconsciously with Mount Pico, the mid-Atlantic volcano in the Azores, which rises 27,000 feet above the bottom of the Atlantic Ocean.

But I am sure of *one* thing — if I lived there I was an independent thinker, endeavoring to communicate directly with the higher powers of the universe, not subject to any school of earthlings.

Also, today I could not imagine myself asking for any other background for any future life. This type of seeking and thinking seems to be ingrained in my innermost being. My father-in-law was Hugenot also, and so our children must have asked for something like an independent thinker's atmosphere.

Chapter XII
Several Theories

WHITHER?
Some of us may be
Shooting stars
Wild —
Storming through the universe
From Sun to Sun,
Fragments of an exploding Nova.

Speeding along
Intergalactic spaceways,
Barely obeying
Traffic laws universal,
Speed limits set
By the Creator.

Others in peaceful orbits
Like Asteroids circling
Our local Sun.

C.T.E.

"You are gods in your inmost parts,
Atoms of some spiritual sun."

Dr. Gottfried de Purcker

(1) THE ASTEROID OR PLANETOID THEORY

So far, we have only a few working theories, perhaps a good start for some metahistorical research to follow.

The thesis to be proven, or to be disproven, is that our essential entities, or beings, may be moving about in definite orbits or patterns, some speeding on hyperbolic tracks like comets through the universe; some even more erratic like shooting stars or meteors, but most others in more stabilized, elliptic patterns like asteroids. They would be in either case subject to the influence of other heavenly, physical or metaphysical bodies.

There is an astronomical theory that a large planet between Jupiter and Mars was destroyed, eons ago by collision or exploded through gravitational pull of Jupiter, resulting in the existence in the orbits between Mars and Jupiter of numerous, fairly large, planetoids, and tens of thousands of very small asteroids, plus innumerable minute particles, now circulating in that space between the 2 large planets. The interesting thing about them is that most of them appear to maintain certain qualities of whatever body was there, and particularly the orbit the original planet probably had.

Reincarnating souls might then be compared to the asteroids, separate particles of an original common source scattered along a common main orbit, but each having its separate identity, size, shape, characteristics and place.

The idea of certain individuals, or even entire groups of people being together repeatedly in different lives is not new, but has not been explored as fully as such a fascinating subject might warrant. We saw why in Chapter III.

Thus, I invite you to share this fascinating project with me. It is a large untilled field.

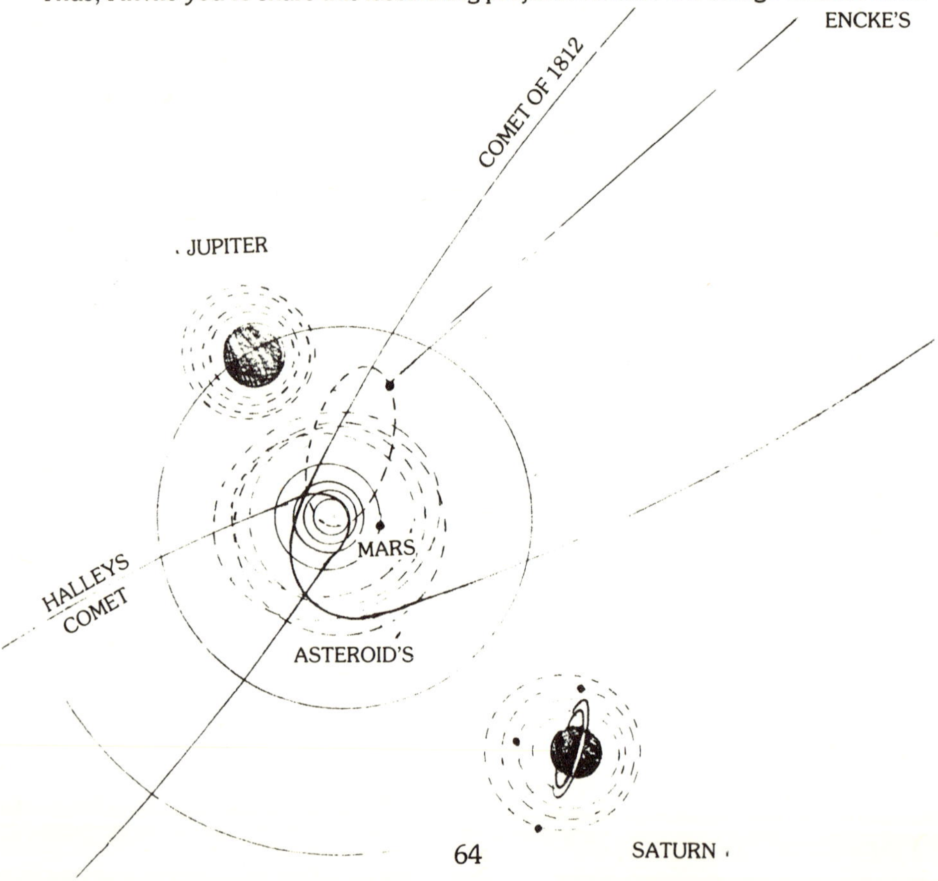

(2) THE NOVA THEORY

There is the old story about several inmates of an insane asylum who simultaneously claimed to be reincarnations of Napoleon (I), and who as a consequence called each other "crazy!" This story was especially relished by people who were prejudiced against the theory of reincarnation and were pleased to recount the story of reincarnation and were pleased to recount the story to prove the "absurdity" of reincarnation. A psychologist M.D. friend of mine tells me that nowadays inmates often imagine themselves as being Hitler, Stalin or Roosevelt.

Being a walking question mark myself (so my parents told me) since the age of less than 2 years, I have been asking myself about this story from time to time, as about many other enigmas in connection with reincarnation. I came upon an hypothesis in an obscure publication that might fit these facts, although it is far from proving anything. Some people have supported this theory, some have denounced it as being absurd.

It is related to the fact that in astronomy there exists a theory of "exploding" Nova stars.

Might there be a parallel here? As above, so below. When a personality ceases to exist on this plane, perhaps having outgrown the necessity of going through reincarnation any further, or perhaps in other cases exploding owing to its own megolomania, it could be split up by the force of a metaphysical explosion into innumerable small entities or soul personalities, with some of its characteristics still clinging, and continuing to cling, to the fragments.

This hypothesis would amongst other things help to explain the frequently advanced quandary of apparent imbalance of numbers of "soul shells" and occupying units whether we choose to call them souls, spirits, entities, atma or ka.

If we adopt the Nova Hypothesis, it would be easier to understand that we feel strongly attracted by different great spirits of the past without pretending to equal them in any way. I personally feel very much akin to the thoughts philosophy and personality of Francis Bacon and Goethe, but do not pretend to be a reincarnation of either one, and incidentally, also much prefer the language of Shakespeare or Schiller. Of course, we may simply have absorbed much of these great people's writings, rather than having inherited even a minute fraction of their souls.

I can relate an experience of a friend of mine who is an excellent artist. This artist has some striking similarities in her style of drawing and painting to that of Albrecht Duerer, the mediaeval German painter. She not only paints in his style and quality, but even seems to choose the same subjects. There is more to it than having been exposed to his works in art school. Was there a genetic nuclear explosion behind this? This closely parallels the "Big Bang" hypothesis of astronomers. Dr. G. de Purucker says: "Ye are gods in inmost parts, atoms of some spiritual sun." All souls are created by one big explosion by, or of, the Creator.

(3) COSMIC OCEAN THEORY

There is a theory that the Cosmic Ocean was created by condensation from the second day of creation. From this ocean vapors arise and, rising into cooler altitudes, condense and finally return to the surface of the planet as fog, air or snow, and fertilize the earth. Transcendentally, this development closely parallels the "Water Cycle" of our physical nature. I believe this was Thomas Edison's favorite theory of reincarnation.

It is interesting to see that Helen Wambach, the well known researcher, writer and teacher of reincarnation, had a dream describing exactly this experience.

A similar tenet is in *The Upanishads*, sacred book of East India, according to which souls return to the earth as rain, to fertilize it.

WATER CYCLES

Drifting snow,
driving rain,
falling angels,
—endless chain.

Reborn spring
on mountainside;
playing waters
leap and glide.

Tumbling waters,
falling brook,
spires of pines,
—a quiet nook.

Running waters,
salmon stream;
through the foliage
sunrays gleam.

River flowing
to the sea,
where transition
sets it free.

C.T.E.

Chapter XIII
Civilizations Reborn

In all living things there is a strong, dominating urge to LIVE. The tiny, fragile seedlings we transplant from the seed box into the garden somehow survive the shock of being transplanted and become flourishing plants. Life may sometimes hang on a thread, or so it seems, and yet innately it is not to be extinguished easily.

I was impressed with the tenacity of a living thing to hang on to dear life when a young orange tree in our garden made a comeback after being taken for dead. It flourished beautifully during its first growing season, but was hard hit by winter frosts and to all appearances had no life left in it. Surprisingly, after being cut back and cared for a bit, it put forth new growth and flourished again.

Likewise, tree stumps will persist in sending up shoots. We had some unwanted acacia trees cut down but the stumps stubbornly persisted in growing, in spite of the axe, and poison, and hard words.

Civilizations seem to act that way, too. If a nation has established solid roots and brought forth worthwhile economic and cultural achievements, some of their heirs, physical or spiritual, will remember them, and it will not die easily. Out of the roots will spring new life.

Leo Frobenius, the German archaeologist, has written besides his dozens of books on archaeology, several books on the lives of nations, more specifically African civilizations. Orthodox scientists do not accept his premise that nations can live and be reincarnated, and so tried to belittle him, finding small faults and errors in his work, unwilling to acknowledge that he had a larger horizon than they did.

Today, it is more or less general knowledge that civilizations disappear and later on reappear in a different "body." Are not the Americans called "the new Romans?" We are comparing many details such as their highway building and the moral decay of the 2 civilizations, and their democratic systems.

Much has been written and spoken about the theory of reincarnation, or rebirth, of nations, yet the parable of the flowering tree stump points out that there is considerable evidence in nature for this principle of renascence.
Educated Romans tried to be as "Greek" as they could because the Greek civilization was considered to be the acme. Even Julius Caesar's famous words: "The die has been cast," were not spoken in Latin, but in Greek.

Greek slaves, highly educated, became teachers of young Romans of good families. Undoubtedly, under their influence rough and ready, clean and strong Rome, after just a few generations, became the civilizator of all of western Europe — but in the process lost its integrity and its strength.

The Freeing of 40,000 German slaves worked like a blood transfusion, but of course made the empire slowly but steadily less "Roman." The slaves who were given their freedom became soldiers and very many officers.

The frontier defenses, by now chiefly relying on alien and minority recruits, soon succumed to other invading Germanic tribes that broke through the eastern and northern frontiers. Soon, these tribes in turn were subverted by and converted to the superior civilization of the subdued Romans, and there emerged from the ruins of the Roman state new ideas and even ideals. Rome was reincarnated in several Germanic physical bodies, although these themselves were not conscious of the process, except perhaps Theodoric the Great. In any case the name of the empire was not revived — not yet!

This was left for the next act on the stage of the western world: CAROLUS MAGNUS, better known as Charlemagne. His Frankish court had become the center of a general cultural revival of civilization in many aspects, and when Pope Leo III finally crowned him in Rome as "Imperator," they created by this action the "Holy Roman Empire of the German Nation," which certainly constituted a rebirth of the Roman Empire, and for the first time since the Caesars included a realm that approached the extent of the old western Roman Empire, reaching from northern Spain to the Baltic Sea, comprising all of France most of Italy and Germany.

Several of the later German emperors, especially Frederic I and Frederic II, may also lay claim to having revived the old spirit and they did use the name. However, the next and almost universal rebirth was one more of art, literature and science, architecture: the Renaissance (the French word for the original Italian RINASCIMIENTO or re-birth). It was a most wonderful flowering of the old tree stumps and roots of antiquity, in which the popes — after all — had not completely extinguished all life, although during the Dark Ages all except religious art had been proscribed.

Again and again, western nations went back to classical sources. Our nearest example is our national capital. We sent for the famous French architect, L'Enfant, to design it and it certainly is a revival of classical architecture. The same style was continued even much later, to cite just one instance, in the Lincoln Memorial, and innumerable other specimens of our new Dorian-American style.

The idea of nations reborn is much more popular with the general public than that of reincarnation of individuals. Perhaps it is because it has been mentioned so often in public statements, whereas individual reincarnation has been a taboo subject for 1500 years in the Western world generally.

A few more examples often cited are: Europe shown as the new Greece, with the sequel of Europe culturally influencing America as Greece influenced Rome.

Britain, the naval power, is cast in the role of Athens, the seafaring nation. Germany, the land power, cast as Sparta, and France as highly sophisticated Corinth.

In addition to those hypothetical revivals of old social and political structures, there have been many that were unsuccessful attempts, some even just wishful thinking. When Napolean I said that he "was Charlemagne," he was not far off. Charles de Gaulle did not get that far with this same idea.

Hitler's THIRD REICH could almost have succeeded if his early successes had not gone to his head and made him lose all sense of reality. Mussolini's revival of the Roman Empire almost succeeded too, with Rome re-established in north and east Africa, and across the Adriatic Sea, had he not been dragged down by Hitler's collapse, because he had tried to cut himself in on part of the loot.

It would take a whole set of books to deal with the study of how the pendulum of history swings, or the tong on the scales of eternal justice, but I cannot resist a quick glance at British History cycles. This is not to discuss karmic guilt or reward, simply statistics on the AGE OF BRITAIN:

1066 - Battle of Hastings

+144 +5 = 1215 - Magna Carta;

+144 __11 = 1358 - Peasants' revolt in France, which gave the signal for a similar movement in England in 1381;

+144 +7 = 1509 - Henry VIII, King of England;

+144 −4 = 1649 - Charles I executed;

+144 −4 = 1789 - George Washington, President of USA;

+144 − 6 = 1939 - Britain declares war on Germany, sealing demise of British Empire.

The theory of the 144 +/− average cycle is still a theory that has to be proven and the dates which really are the turning points may be others such as Cromwell's accession or the Declaration of Independence, or the Boston Tea Party ...but there seems to be enough of a periodicity to be studied.

Let's now have a closer look at the center of the continent. Why did Germany invade France successfully 4 times within less than 144 years? (1814, 1870, 1914, 1940)

In 1672 Louis XIV invaded Germany; in 1681 he took Strassburg; in 1689 he destroyed Heidelberg.

143 years later, 1815, Prussia (with the help of Russia and Austria) took Paris.

1756-1763 (Sevens Years' War) Louis XVI made war in Germany.

+144 +7 = 1914, Germany invaded France.

1805 Napoleon invaded Germany (he took Berlin in 1806)

+144 −8 = 1941 - Germany invaded France.

Wars have been fought over the Rhine river for roughly 2000 years, and the above examples show swings of the pendulum.

We should mention in passing that the 144-year-cycle very frequently appears in the history of nations, and that the underlying principle of Karma compensation frequently takes place through the very factors which made the nation incur karmic debts.

It should also be noted that preliminary study seems to show that:

(1) Nobody has been guiltless;
(2) Nobody escapes the judgments of the Supreme Court of the Cosmos;
(3) Nobody seems to have learned the simple lesson: cause and effect.
(4) Nobody seems to have been rehabilitated in the "Correctional Facilities" (to express it in modern legal terms).

Our above excursions into the field of Serial Lives of Kingdoms, such as invasion, occupation, deportation, exile in captivity, repeated holocausts may not prove much if anything, but I cannot refrain from citing one more striking example for the cycles!

Charlemagne, the 1st Emperor of the "Roman Empire of the German Nation" began his rule as King of the Franks in 768, and the last Emperor of Germany, Wilhelm II, finished his reign with his abdication in 1918, so the Empire lasted with some interruptions 1150 years, almost exactly 8 cycles of 144 years each.

Is the figure of 144 years an essential feature in the life of a nation, or civilization? It does seem to make it interesting to pursue statistical research along these lines.

Part II
Voyages Into Time

"Knowledge is a form of recollection."
—Plato

HERE are:
Some poems,
—probably the purest form of recalls;
Some letters,
—more from a conscious level;
Some quotations,
—from third parties;
Some experiences,
—of friends;
Some unadorned dates from history.

I hope that some of them may serve as points of departure for meditative travel in inner space.

INTO TIME

No, thank you,
Your Multinational Majesty,
We won't need your Lear Jet,
Not even your Rolls —
Or your Constellation —
They are out-dated.
Where could they take us?
Into Space?
Through Time? — —
Let's go and see
My old friend Vasco.
Da Gama will gladly
Lend us an old caravel!
It will do nicely
As our magic carpet.
After all, Vasco succeeded
Where Columbus had failed.
Come to my realm
Under the Space Dome.
Let us look down
Into palace and hovel.
Harun al Rashid!
I'll be your vizir
For 101 nights —
Now close your eyes
And open your mind,
Listen with care:
Is it the wind
In our lateen sails?
Or could it be
The Music of Spheres???

A FRIEND AT COSNA* *(15,000 B.C.)*

I do not understand
The lines you use,
But read the message
Clearly written
Between your lines:
"PAJAROS COLOR ACERO,"
Spaceships alighting
On the sky port of Nazca,
Cosmonauts calling,
Calling you home …

Your ear has forgotten
The language they speak,
Which you spoke long ago,
Not SO long, after all …
It will now be tuned
To their transmission,
"COSMOPUERTO NAZCA."

You want to go home,
But it is not for Chile
You are yearing —
It's even beyond Peru.
El Pajaro Color Acero
Is waiting at Nazca
To lift you to join
La reina de los
Angeles Cosmonautas.

Pajaro Color Acero,
The steel colored bird.
Easy in English,
Yet given in Spanish,
While they are switching
Your radar channel
To your grandmother tongue,
Before Spanish.

COSmopuerto Interplanetario de NAzca

ARAUCANIA * *(13000 B.C.)*

Araucanians, ARA UC Arians,
Hittites' and Castilians' brothers
From another, outer planet,
Floating TransPacific rafts
To the mystery of Easter Island,
To Juan Fernandez' Mas a Tierra,
'Yond the Galapagos even,
Where DEUS EX MACHINA * *
Pulled history's final curtain
Upon another Mystery.

---

  * *Region of Chile and South Pacific Islands.*
* * *Ancient Greek Stage Effect:*
   "Divine intervention from the wings."

YUCATAN

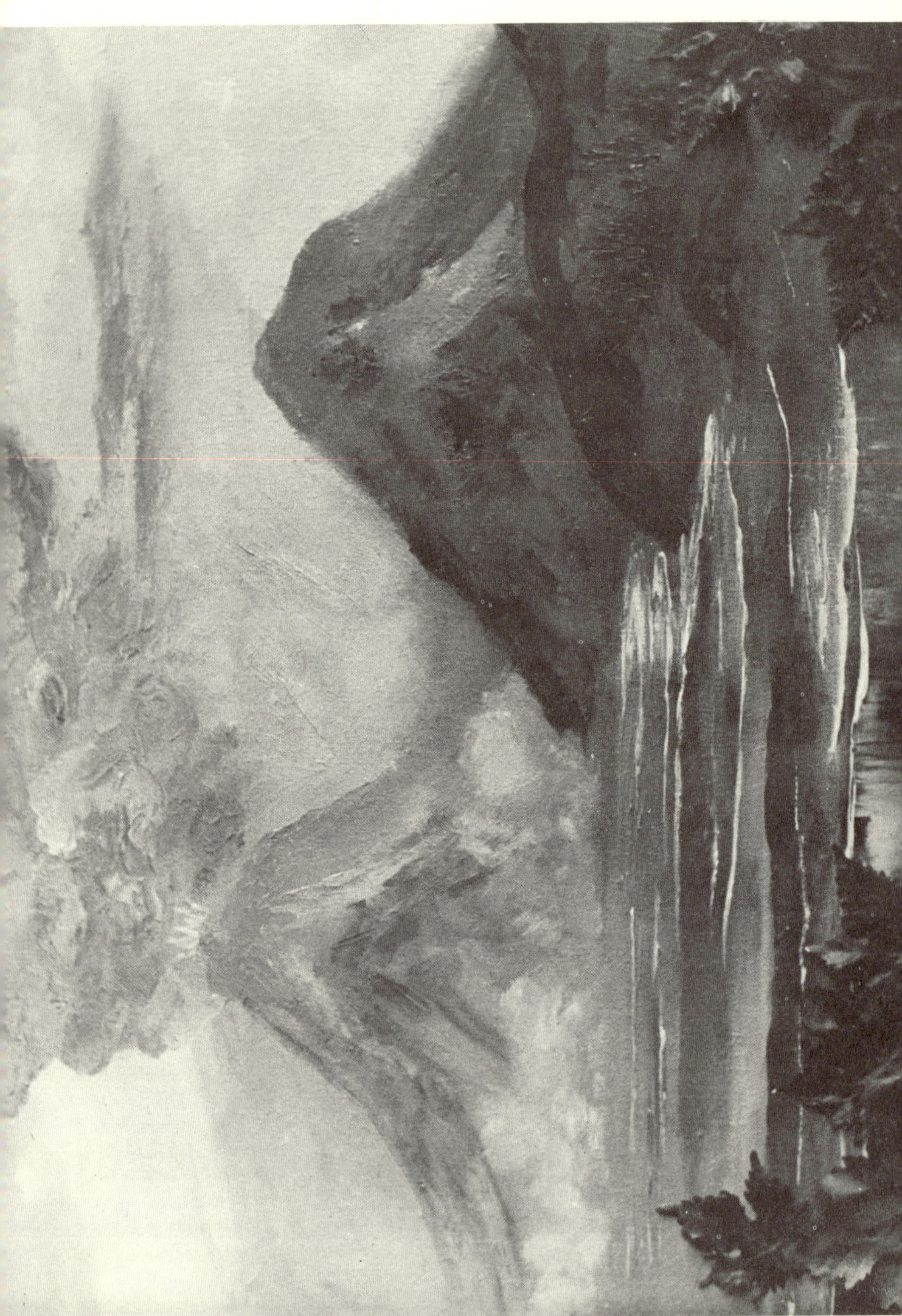

FORTUNATE ISLES
(8500 B.C. — 1980 A.D.)

Gazing at the Magic Mountain,
Relaxing in the sunshine,
Thankful for every day;
Reclining ... into a dream?

* * *

I seen to be sitting
On one of the Ilhas Afortunadas,
In mid-Atlantic,
Truly the "Isles of the Blessed." *
Now, souvenirs
Are welling up
Under the veils
Of centuries.

Etna, Pico Alto and Pico de Teide
Appear strongly in memory,
Fuji San just a mirror
That reflects them ...
Palenque, Uxmal,
Chicken Itza,
Were household words
From earliest childhood.

When I was five, I drew
Sketches of Castle Pena,
Where friends saw me imprisoned
Five hundred years after the fact.

Faithfully I had
Served the Infante, **
But when he died
That was held against me.
Good friends helped me
Escape to Ultramar,
Madeira ... and thence,
Later, the Acores.

---

* *Ilhas Afortunadas (Acores, Madeiras, Canarias, Cap Verde), thus named by the ancients because of their ideal climate, growing fruit not yet found in the prehistoric Mediterranean. Were they perhaps also called thus because they were the only surviving mountain tops, when Atlantis collapsed?*

** *Voyage to Gondwana pages 72-87.*

There I received the news
That my friend Bartolomeu
Now was disgraced at Court,
And Vasco given command.
I heard Vasco sailed and sailed
And opened wide sea lanes
To Calicut, Cochin,
And Cannanore …
Oh, how I wished that I
Could draw his charts
The way I did at Vila do Infante
For Cao and Bartolomeu …

Mount Pico Alto seems peaceful now,
But it still looks like Atlas
Carrying the weight of heaven
On his shoulders:
His inverted pyramid of smoke,
10,477 years**
After the Asteroid blew up Atlantis.

* * *

…That shock woke me up!
But, am I truly awake?
I still see a graceful volcano
Rising behind my grapevines,
But there is no column of smoke …

Am I awake or asleep?
I turn on the cold shower,
But it comes hot from the tap:
That volcano is real!
Though it seems to be sleeping—
It must be Mount Saint Helena!

So I am sitting here
On a different "isle of the blessed"—
Fortunate Alta Napa …
Thankful for every single day.

** *According to the Mayan Calendar records transposed into our Gregorian Calendar, it was at 12:00 O'clock, on June 5th, 8498 B.C. This date is corroborated by approximation by Professor Libby's C-14 tests at Folsom, Texas, and others.*

Where were you?
in the early afternoon
June 5th, 8498 B.C.
(Gregorian Calendar)

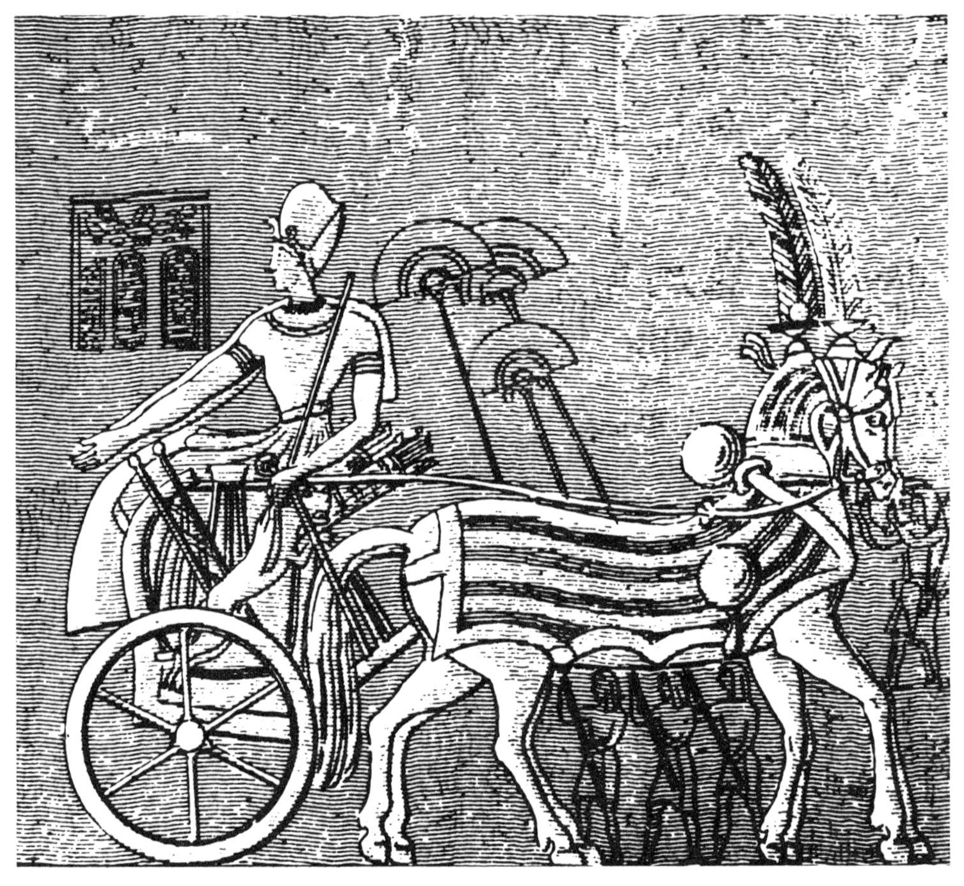

BY THE NILE (1370 B.C.)

When I pulled the reins,
Two white horses reared.
They pranced and they neighed.
Two little girls cheered.

Two little girls smiling
When I drove them to school
By the Temple,
Not far from the Nile.

Princesses of Egypt —
Wilful and wistful —
All full of joy —
Often in trouble
In play, or in ploy.

To be their groom
Was no easy task,
To drive them home
Out of mischief —
But I loved it …

P.S. I was an Ethiopian slave, but had quite a nice job.

ΑΘΗΝΑΙ

ATHENS

466—449 B.C. Pericles
431—404 B.C. Peloponnesian War
401   The "Long March" of the 10,000
469—399 B.C. Socrates

Where were YOU in those days?

Where did our roads cross?

P.S. I was there, but just as an ordinary Greek sailor on the regular runs to Sicily, and other ports of Magna Graecia, so you probably would not remember me.

R.S.V.P.

WHITE CLIFFS OF LEUKAS
(370 B.C.)

As the noon sun strikes
The white cliffs of Leukas,
It is lifting the veil
Of fog from the dreaming
Ionian Sea,
As the Bireme carries me home,
Home from Athens,
Home from Zakynthos.

Leukas seems still as it was
When Leukothea gently
Carried Odysseus ashore
On the soft white cushions,
The foam of her breakers.

Where the guiltless invoked
Apollo Leukatas
To absolve them of crime,
And lovers, too, took
The "Leukadian leap"
Fifty yards down,
And amidst the rocks
Into the boiling sea.

Some did survive,
But it surely was
The final cure
For love-sickness.

So it had been
In Mykenian time,
And before Amxichi
And Nidhri were built.

So it was now — and the cliffs
Called me back to my home,
Acarnania —
The bright shining cliffs on Leukas.

Did YOU know:

POSEIDONIOS?

Born in 135 B.C., in Apameia, Syria,
died in 50 B.C. on Rhodos,
pupil of Panaetis of the Plato-Aristotle School,
researched in Spain (Cadiz!), Sicily, Italy, and
other Mediterranean shores,
finally settled as a well known teacher in Rhodes.

P.S. Did we meet in his school on the Island of Rhodos?   *R.S.V.P.*

MARE NOSTRUM* — 134 A.D.

A wispy haze was hovering over the water. Salty sea air was drifting in from the Mediterranean, with the tangy smell of sea moss, and little wavelets were washing white strings of pearly bubbles over the dark, wet sands, as we were waiting ... waiting on the shore west of Alexandria ... waiting, scanning the horizon. What were we waiting for? Who were we waiting for?

We were Jews of the Essene sect who had escaped the holocaust of the Jews in Cyrenaica, west of Egypt, and had found temporary shelter near Alexandria ... refugees ... waiting. What were we waiting for? We were waiting for a ship to appear over the horizon, a fast Roman bireme, the imperial courier ship "Astraea," that was due to arrive and would probably bring us some news about the situation in Palestine. To go into Alexandria meant risking our very lives, even though some of our group still were sheltered there.

There had been many new developments in the Roman Empire since Trajan, the conqueror, had died in Selinus, on his way home to Rome, tragically stricken with a fatal illness right after his conquest of the lands beyond the Euphrates.

We had been full of hope. We knew that his successor, his nephew Hadrian, was a peace-maker. He had almost immediately, personally, turned Parthia back to its king. He felt it was useless to bleed the empire in constant wars against the Parthians. Old legionnaires were being released to their home countries, and new legionnaires were being recruited locally. Our Spanish-born emperor was certainly changing the course of politics, building, conserving: tax relief for the citizens, social security for poor children. He was building a huge wall right across Scotland — a frontier, beyond which he did not want to go, leaving the Scots alone if they would leave the Romans in peace. Building on the continent too, consolidating, establishing peace everywhere.

Yes, peace everywhere — except in Palestina, where the Zealots were once more rebelling. How often had the holy city and the temple been defiled, burned, desecrated, taken by force of arms? It was hard to count. Surely one of the most contested sanctuaries in history.

Hadrian was establishing law and order everywhere in the empire — even in North Africa, which had been devasteded and depopulated in the fierce Jewish revolt in Cyrenaica — everywhere but in Palestina. Of course, we Jews, or rather some of our brethren, had not made it easy for him, but some corrupt administrators had driven the Zealots to despair. Now Hadrian, the great peace-maker, had made his one great historical mistake. On the ruins of destroyed Jerusalem, he decided to build a new capital for Palestina: Aelia Capitolina. The ruins had been abandoned since Titus destroyed the city. Our great humanitarian — the artist, the writer, the friend of scholars, the initiate of the mysteries — had failed to understand the simple minds of an over-proud, stubborn people, willing to die for their convictions, even if the struggle was completely hopeless. Broadminded and well meaning, he did not realize that this apparently constructive action would fan the ashes, that seemed to have cooled, into a new firestorm of rebellion, more devastating than any before. Apparently his secret service, typical Roman, thick-skinned, squareheads, had not warned him, probably did not even realize themselves, that erecting this "Aelia Capitolina" with a huge new temple to Jupiter Capitolinus, on the ashes of Jerusalem, would have a disastrous effect by driving the Jews, even though they were completely beaten, into a new frenzied wave of revolt — regardless of the consequences which they on their part also could have easily foreseen, had they been able to reason coolly.

These few bands of fanatics, unwilling to compromise with the world power that had so recently conquered the entire western world from Spain to the Euphrates, and

---

Mare Nostrum = Our Sea = The Roman Sea = The Mediterranean.

from Britain to Africa — these Zealots — were plainly asking for another Masada tragedy. We, the peaceful, perhaps too peaceful Essenes could not stop our brothers and were caught between two fires.

For two years already the guerilla-war had been waged, leaving Cyrenaica and Palestina completely prostrated, and even Alexandria severely damaged, but we were still hoping that the two parties would see the light. Waiting ... waiting ... we were waiting here in the year 134 A.D., hoping against hope for favorable news, as many of our relatives were involved in the fighting as Zealot guerillas. Some others, more Hellenized, or should we say Romanized, would pass the news on to us. One of the officers on the courier ship was a friend and would send us word. Some of our co-religionists had found refuge in the Hoggar and in the Fezzan. We would soon have to decide in which direction to flee. A few of our people still appeared to be fairly safe inside Alexandria, but that could change any minute.

P.S. It did — for the worse. Many of our people died in the Colosseum.

SARI'S SONG

When first I heard the name of "Sari"
Two years ago, it struck a gong.
It touched me deeper than I knew
How to explain, for then I knew no Sari,
Nor you, and did not realize that once
It meant so much to me, so long ago,
When Sari sang that age-old song,
That melody I always knew,
That harmony that has descended
Through many centuries for us.

But it was just two days ago
I realized this melody was you.

* * *

SARI AT THE WELL
(India — 700 A.D.)

Do you remember Kalamari?
The tropic sun on its adobe walls?
Do you remember when I called you "Sari,"
The Banyan tree behind the village well?

Under its branches, cool and quiet,
Deep in your eyes, so soft and dark,
Were moments of supreme delight
In calm and quiet happiness.

But time was short,
I made you stay too late —
Your mother called, the spell was broken,
And that is all that I remember now.

* * *

DONAR THE PARSON
(920A.D. — 1920A.D.)

Thor Donar, the Thunderer,
Launched from the Nordic Coast
His longships to Scotland
With the Viking host.

He hurled "Thor's Hammer":
Viking Commandos from longships,
His grandson thundered the fear
Of the new god from pulpits.

Donald, the preacher,
The pagan's teacher —
By Pherson, the parson,
Donar Thor was forgot.

Or did he maintain
In his innermost heart
Admiration and awe
For his forebear?
He sailed from Thule to Vinland and China,
He roamed in the wake of the Viking,
Never lost his love of the sea.

Staunch friends will soon hear him,
With bagpipes in Valhall,
Cheering the Valkyries on
With songs of ships and the sea.

P.S. Reincarnations of my friend, Donald McPherson.

PALERMO (1200 A.D.)

Panormus Palermo,
The Western World's center —
Constance d'Hauteville,
Federigo von Stauffen,
Norman and German,
Spanish and Greek —
Not to forget the Phoenicians,
Sikulers, Arabs and Carthaginians,
Even a dash of the Romans:
Descendents of Troy.
More Greek than Latin it was,
In spirit at least.
Magna Graecia's Last Capital —
Amongst the intrigues
At the court, and
Between Pope and Empire
We were dancing like cats
On a hot tin roof.
A dangerous job
To be district attorney,
Loyal to d'Hauteville
And Hohenstaufen —
Law and order to keep
Was no child's play.
Many a man we sent
To the sulfur mines near the sea.
Because he betrayed us to Rome.
Heartbreaking job —
And seven centuries later
I met some that I had hurt. *

———————————

* *P.S. In France and U.S.A.*
See page 24.

SOUVENIRS d'ALBI (A.D. 1213)

Ne comprenant bien l'Occitan,
Il va falloir te parler en francais,
Pour retrouver les lieux que tu aimais,
Car a Toulouse je n'ai pas réussi,
Non plus à Avignon, ni même Albi.
As tu seulement quitte ton île
Pour écumer les mers qui baignent la Sicile?

Te souviens tu de St Trophime, — Narbonne,
N'as tu pas vu de près les tours de Carcassonne?
N'en as tu jamais fait la ronde
Aux temps de la duchesse Esclairemonde, —
Mais, Blanchefleur, cela est sur:
Tu as connu le Duc Raymond et — Montségur.

DE BRUG in BRUGGE
(A.D. 1330)

I still cannot forget
That small bridge in Brugge
Over the old canal.

I was the heretic
The crowd had chased,
Stirred up by the priests,
And now brought to bay
Alongside the gracht.

The stones came flying —
One hit my temple —
So it was all over,
Almost before it started.

BRUGGE

Brugge is what its inhabitants call it. To Americans, it is better known by its French name, Bruges. It is a city of bridges and canals, the Venice of the North. It still has preserved the spirit of its mediaeval grandeur of the 13th century when it was the chief commercial center of northwestern Europe. This was before London and Amsterdam took over, after Brugge's river to the sea silted up beyond repair.

Today, Brugge would seem to be an appropriate home for a Sleeping Beauty, dreaming of her golden past, but it has been discreetly yet effectively re-gilded through the trade of the tourists now flocking to this showpiece of northwestern Europe.

My wife and I had both been strongly attracted subconsciously to Brugge. We had already made several, what we called spring-pilgrimages to enjoy the fairytale canals, bridges, canoes and boats, and horse carriages. We had "done" all the tourist show places from the "Beguinage of the Vineyards" to the churches, the Chapel of the Holy Blood, the Belfry and the mansions of the old wool tycoons. We had enjoyed watching the graceful swans glide over the silent waters from the dining room windows of the hostelry, the "Duc de Bourgogne."

Almost by accident we heard there was here in Brugge a replica of the Church of the Holy Sepulchre in Jerusalem. On checking the tourist guide books, we found it almost ignored. The clerk at the hotel, where we had been sleeping in Napoleon's bed, could not tell us how to get there.

I decided that if I HAD lived here several centuries ago, as I believed,I could find it regardless. I started out without a map in the early evening, heading away from the tourist center, thinking that if it had been there we would surely have seen it. So I headed toward the opposite end of the town, to the northeast, following my intuition, and sure enough, it did not take me more than about half an hour to find the church.

In spite of the late hour,the deacon kindly opened the door and put on the lights for me. The church, which had appeared small and unassuming from the outside, was however quite impressive inside, an architectural masterpiece, in spite of its small size.

I remember very impressive flags lined up in the upper part of the side nave of the church. They were supposed to be flags of the crusaders' times, but the church was burnt down once and restored, and possibly only one of the flags was saved. Incidentally, the original Church of the Holy Sepulchre in Jerusalem burnt down several times and is by now probably far removed from the original, after which ths one in Brugge was supposed to be fashioned.

The church in Brugge was built by the brothers Peter and James Adornes, who had vowed to build it in their home town if they returned alive from the crusades in Palestine.

In the crypt of the church is a replica of the supposed original burial vault, with a replica of the crucified body in it.

The next day I tried it again in daylight, with a map I had finally managed to get hold of. I was amazed that I had found it at all the first time. Anyone familiar with the layout of Brugge — its maze of canals, winding streets and bridges that one had to cross — will agree it was amazing. I could see from the map that I had walked there almost by the shortest direct route possible and had taken some half-dozen right and left turns, and bridges, absolutely necessary to get there.

This confirmed my conviction that I had lived in Brugge in the Middle Ages.

FLORENCE 1500 A.D.

Dear Leo,

How stupid of me, Leo, to ask you, last week: "WHEN?"

Of course, it was about 1500, and Florence had only recently become a real democracy!!! Did you have a hand in that?

Incidentally, I saw Pietro's wife. She told me that Pietro flew to Florence especially *just* to attend the 500th birthday of Michelangelo in 1975.

Pietry was a real Renaissance man, who almost lived in the Renaissance now!

Der Jagdflieger war aber anscheinend nicht Dir gegenüber bei Anzio, sondern an der Ostfront! Maybe he was one of our great Pal Cesare Borgia's men? And, of course, please pardon my faux pas in linking you to a Roman Emperor "X" — whereas you so clearly were much closer to Pope Leo X. Do you have a picture of him? I suspect you were a chip off the old block.

Did we meet at your brother Giuliano's house in Firenze?

Siempre mejor!

(Migliore! to you.)
Carlo

FLORENCE (1500 A.D.)

What was I doing
In suddenly, newly
Democratized
Firenze?

We had to hide an old friend —
Though he was one of Cesare's men.

Giuliano was the only one
That could help us;
He knew Pietro was a good man,
Who had helped you, Leo, to rise.

   Giulio's mansion was bright
With the lights for a party,
And with the guests
Coming and going,
We could slip Pietro
Quickly into the house —
And up the broad marble stairs —
Finally into the attic.

Nobody would suspect
That Guiliano would harbor
A fugitive from
The new-dreaded council
Of the Republic.

... M I S S E D ...

(1976 A.D.)

He went too soon,
I came too late !
Zu frueh ?
Zu spaet !
Trop tard
trop tot …
Wie oft,
She sobbed …
How often ?
Souvent !
Too late
Zu spaet !
Er ging zu frueh,
Il est parti,
Nous sommes ici —

Nature alas
Knows of no waiting …

To the memory of my friend

The POET
Peter Becker
Oakville von Eichendorff

COMO

I experienced another instance of spontaneous recall when I was about 22 years old. It happened in Como, the age-old Roman city at the head of beautiful Lake Como, in the Italian Alps.

My friend Theo's mother and sister and I arrived by train on our way from Bremen to Rome. Usually in European cities in those days it was a safe bet that one could get rooms in one of the hotels surrounding the railroad stations.

However, it was the height of the tourist season and there was NO VACANCY. I asked a taxi driver if he could find us some rooms somewhere in the city. "No," he said, "everything is taken."

Suddenly an idea flashed through my head —

"Stay here with the luggage," I said to my friends, "I think I know of a place." The taxi driver repeated there was nothing, but I asked him to drive me toward the northeast of the city along the quays. After about 10 blocks, I said, "Now turn right." There were certainly no hotels, or restaurants or commercial buildings in this section, just residences and a few old warehouses. However, after about 2 blocks I saw a small sign on the left side of the street: "TRATTORIA DEL AGNELLO" "Inn of the Lamb."

The inn was probably 400 years old at least, but it looked well maintained and was very clean inside. They had 2 large rooms, very plain but spotless, with sandstone tile floors. No rugs. ("Just as well," I thought.)

I went back to the depot and fetched my friends. We had supper at the inn, plain and substantial, but tasty, and we had a very good night's rest until 2 energetic roosters in the courtyard announced morning was nigh. Looking out of the window, I saw them strutting about on top of the neatly piled dung-heap — in the middle of the central courtyard, around which the buildings were constructed! It was just a typical medieval European or near eastern inn or caravanserai. No, there were no fleas or bedbugs! I was glad my sophisticated lady friends, city ladies from Bremen did not inspect the courtyard before turning in that night. Como was the famed silk capital of Italy and next day they visited Moretti's and a few other elegant wholesale silk yardage houses. I appreciated the contrast.

I must have stayed there several hundred years before. This time it was a very pleasant experience.

ANTONIO VENEZIANO
1543—1593 Palermo

In Sicily, as earlier in Italy, academies were established to cultivate literature and poetry. The first one was the Academia degli Accesi in Palermo, under the auspices of the Spanish viceroy in 1551; many writers were members of it. However, there was amongst them only one real poet, who later on was given the honorary title of "Master and Prince of Sicilian Poetry."

He was Antonio Veneziano, born in Monreale in 1543. His fame spread throughout Italy as a wonder of scholarship, since he wrote poetry in 4 languages: Latin, Spanish, Toscano (the "Italian" to be), and the local idiom: Siciliano. In this language had been written the first verses in the tongue of the people, but it was pushed aside for a long time as written language, by Latin.

But with the advent of the poetry of Antonio Veneziano, Siciliano was given back its rights as a language of poets. Veneziano wrote spiritual as well as worldly songs, canzones and epigrams; he published a collection of Sicilian proverbs and wrote a symbolism of colors in terzarimas or terzines. He was renowned for his ingenious wit.

Politicians feared him, as he was not afraid to attack the government; however he was jailed for this and met his death in chains in a tower of Castellamare near Palermo in 1593, when it was blown up in a gunpowder explosion.

Ironically, the same viceroy who had thus indirectly caused his death, gave him an honorable ceremonial funeral.

Do you remember his study in Palermo? I hope you did not meet him on that Barbary Coast galley with Cervantes —

P.S.: This is from a report by Dr. Rolf Passer, of Vienna.

A.D.* 1350 — TSINING

Ping — Ting,
Sounds sing
Across the still water —
I can hear the copper smiths'
Hammers dancing and singing,
Singing Ping Ting,
As I leave Tsining.

As the barge glides down
Toward the Grand Canal,
I look back on my
Happy, carefree youth.

I had just returned
To my parents' home —
But the courts were empty,
Empty the sandbox
Where she had played,
My little sister,
Dzao-Tcheh …

I heard she was still alive,
Though far away in Peking;
So I wrote her a letter,
And hope it will reach her.

(Letter follows.)

LAKSPUL
SECOND MONTH, YEAR OF THE BOAR

It is a long time, Little Sister, since we were together in our parents' home in Tsining, but I remember it all very clearly — I can see the central court of our house, with the big sandbox where you used to play while I was watching you. The big weeping willow was already turning to pale yellow in the early fall, but it was still warm enough for us children to play outside, protected in the court from the equinoctial winds that had started to blow down over the TZING HAI; already the sun was a bit pale and the sky was pastel blue.

I remember only one other court, the first court towards the street, where our father would take care of his business and visitors, though there must have been a third one in the back because there was a cook and a house boy and two maids — not many servants as Chinese households go, but we were not rich, just comfortable. Our father went with the silk caravans to Ormuzd, and to Buchara. He made good money, but the trips were long, and on one of his trips, when he made a very good sale in Samarkand, he spent all his profits (and a bit more) in buying that beautiful Cherkessian slave who was to become your mother. I can still remember her, with her wonderfully thick black hair and deep blue flashing eyes! After her initial resistance to the idea of being wed to a Chinese, she settled down very well in our household.

My mother was a Mongolian, much older, and of course not as good looking as your mother, but she accepted her gracefully as the second wife, who in turn was glad to accept the second place in the house — supervising the servants and giving a hand herself against the friendly tutorship she received in return. She was thus made familiar with and at home in a strange country thousands of miles away from her own. Our father never married again, and there were no other children. Your mother treated her step-son very well and there was harmonious family life.

I passed the examina to serve at the court of the Son of Heaven, and went away to Peking. When I came back ten years later, from the war in An-Nam, not only you — Little Sister — were gone, but the house was empty, and there was just the old willow tree weeping in the fall sunshine.I was told DSAO CHE had gone to live with Wah Chang the engineer, to Tientsin, to Peking, even to the Great Wall.

I could not bear to be in Tsining without any of our family so I left for SOOCHOW where I established myself in the Herb, Lotion and Salve business.

Sometimes, I wonder how things are now in TZUNG KUO in general, and in SHANTUNG and KIANGSU in particular.

Younger Sister, do you know what happened to our parents after you left home? I was told by the neighbors that your mother died giving birth to a second child, taking the child with her, and that my mother apparently died of gallstones at about the same time that our father was lost in a sandstorm in the TAKLAMAKAN in Central Asia, where he was traveling as partner in a new silk caravan. I arrived at our home only many months later, having been in distant parts of the empire in the course of my military and administrative duties, in An-Nam, Cochin, Nam-Viet, even the Cardamon Mountains. By the time I got home, our former servants had scattered and nobody knew how to reach you.

I was able to sell the house, as I could not stand the thought of living there, and with the proceeds went to establish my self in business in SOOCHOW. This is all now long ago, although in retrospect it seems like yesterday when we loaded my few possessions on the canal boat. The pale morning sun of the fall day was raising veils of tule fog from the water as the barge slowly started to move. I can still hear the water gently lapping against the sides of the boat and see the drops glistening in the sun as they dripped off the poles. I was very tired, having worked all night to liquidate things. When the barge emerged from the Grand Canal into the boundless expanse of Weishan Hu Lake I fell asleep.

I had travelled a great deal in my work for the government — to Kunming and Chungking, Turkestan and Hainan, even to the Hakka country where (my father told me) his father's father had come from. He did not know more than a very few words of the great Hakka language, even though he talked ABOUT it. I had been to Taiwan, too, and all this travelling had made me weary of travel, and I was content now to stay put in our home provinces.

How often my memory takes me back to our home when we were all happy there together! How well I remember the very dark color of the tiles of my mother's house — they were of an unusual, almost bluish-black, with underlying carmine, different from the other roofs. Perhaps it was the oldest building in the court.

That last time I was there, all I found of you were two beautiful screens, which the neighbors told me you had painted, so you probably must have had some instruction in that. This is all I am able to recall at this time — I do not even remember your given name. You were just DSAO CHE, the Younger Sister in the Liu family. But — AS I WRITE NOW — it comes out PEACH BLOSSOM- Is that correct?

Fond greetings from your Elder Brother,

LIU KHAN.

California, June 1980

I was so proud of you, Little Sister, yesterday — to see you there with your art show in Vallejo. What a fine show! What impressed me most was your painting, "San Francisco Skyline" — done in Chinese style! I liked it the best of any skylines I have seen. If I had had money I would have bought it and taken down one of mine from the wall to make room for it. The second most impressive was the "Gate of the Japanese Tea Garden," also painted in Chinese style — not Japanese!

Wah Chang fitted it well with his Filipino shirt.

You said again that you did not have that deep feeling of kinship for China that you might expect. It struck me that this also fits into the jigsaw puzzle. You were half Cherkess so subconsciously you felt the pull of roots from a different direction, and some resistance to things Chinese. Likewise, my mother was Mongolian so I did not have the deep indwelling love for China that a Han or a Szechuanese might have. I was interested, having been born into it and brought up in it, but always living with some reservations toward its culture. Among my Oriental friends was a Mongolian who always stressed the difference between Mongols and Chinese. You may remember him — the owner of the "Kublai Khan." Another close Chinese friend was from Macao, a member of one of the many minorities that lived on the fringes of the Empire of the Son of Heaven.

During your incarnation in China you received years of lessons in painting, and they seem still to be embedded in your genes.

So, one after the other the transcendental components of the great Chinese jig-saw puzzle seem to fall into place. Maybe Wah Chang could help me. The only things I knew about him in that long-ago life were that he was an engineer, a Buddhist, and a good man. I only met him years later.

As ever, your Elder brother,

Liu Khan

CAUCASIA (1614-1650 Tuapse)

Was it near Sochi,
Or Wladikawkas?
I can still see the last
Rays of the sun
Lingering on the classical
Colonnade of the Manor.
The Grand Duke had gone
To the Court of The Czar.
I was the lowly "POP,"
The priest of the village,
A Kuban Cossack,
And I helped the Duchess,
Xenia Alexeievna,
Keep things under control,
Including myself ...
I can still see her standing
On the terrasse of the long low mansion
And the last rays of the sun
Lingering on ...
In her red-golden hair. —

And well I remember
The shining dark hair
Of my secret sweetheart,
Myrtilla, the blue-eyed Tcherkess.

P.S. It was my job to maintain a "theological insurance" for the Grand Duke's family and estate. I met them again in 1946 in San Francisco. He was still the outwardly genial but very detached master. 34 years later I met their daughter, Sasha, who had played at my feet as a child, a teenager when I left them. I taught her all I knew and she was an excellent student, especially in Latin and history, but she grew up too fast — all of a sudden.

RED LETTER DAYS

The next time you two met again
On Flanders' Fields, in France,
The clouds hung heavy down with rain
And death was leading the dance,
    When they rode and smote as they strode—
    The Four Horsemen of St. John.

Of human rights they talked and made
A charnel of liberty,
They killed in castle, square and glade
In the name of humanity.
    For they smote as they strode and rode
    The Four Horsemen of St. John.

Hand over your home, your wife, and gold!
For the sake of fraternity.
No use to you, once your head has rolled
To establish equality.
    They rode and they smote as they strode
    The Four Horsemen of St. John.

That night when you smiled to the peasant maid—
Did you know she saved your life?
She hid you in the bed she made,
Did not ask to be made your wife.
    And they strode and smote when they rode
    The Four Horsemen of St. John.

When you left in the grey morning's mist
For England—not merry, but old,
She remembered how you had kissed,
And left her a purse of gold.
    So they rode and smote as they strode,
    The Four Horsemen of St. John.

Her parents found out—her life became hell,
The hamlet she left for the town.
Your kisses and gold she remembered well,
In pearls and black satin gown.
    While they rode and smote as they strode,
    The Four Horsemen of St. John.

A.D. 1800 (1758 Rijssel)

Do you see the candles,
Three on the table
In the tavern in Lille …
The pearls you gave me
Are glistening now
On my black velvet gown —
They turned into tears,
Lieutenant, after you left me.
You had stolen the pearls
As you stole my heart.

P.S. I was a blonde born under the Sign of Cancer, and after the above sad beginning became as they say in France, "a daughter of joy."

See page 51 in "Voyage to Gondwana," poem "Red Letter Days."

JUNCTION IN BRITTANY (1938 A.D.)

The Cornouaille—Lorient Limited
From Paris had just stopped
At three o'clock in the morning,
At Auray Junction —
Here in the countryside
The first roosters
Just began to stir.
The farmers that had shown their wares
At the Foire de Paris: cider, applejack,
Famous, fragrant, herb-seasoned
Breton sausages of all kinds,
Were now waiting for the sunrise train
To take them home to their villages.
I was on a pilgrimage to Loc Mariaquer,
The Stonehenge of "Little Britain."

The dark waiting room
Was of moderate size,
Yet loomed large like
An aeroplane hangar —
So quiet at four o'clock
In the morning.
Only the clicking
Of dice that were rolling,
And a farmer teasing
The girls
That were bringing dozens of
Huge cups
Filled with cafe au lait —
Its aroma joined by that
Of the fresh farm bread
Just from the oven,
That was now being passed out.
With butter fresh from the churn,
They cut us thick slices —
We dipped them into the large cups.
The cool air of the night
Had made us hungry,

And I'll never forget the fragrance
Of that tasty,solid farm bread —
Dunked in the giant size cups —
I have tried to duplicate it
Many times since!
So far, never quite made it.
I guess I'll have to return
To Auray Junction
On a June morning at four o'clock.

Postscripta

We can visualize rebirth as a logical explanation of the inequalities of life. Each of us is the restult of his past actions and experiences. Reincarnation shows a universe operating with justice and wisdom.

Without an understanding of THE LAW, life appears frustrating and futile. What reasons could there be for the struggles humans go through on earth, unless the answer is to progress to a higher state, ultimately approaching perfection?

Each rebirth is a new deal for missed opportunities, and for new and greater ones. In each life we learn certain lessons and pay off karmic debts as we earn good point bonuses, fringe benefits on a spiritual level.

One of the most succinct condensations of the whole principle of karma was made by Saint Paul, when he wrote: "Brethren, do not be deceived. God is not mocked — for whatsoever a man soweth, that shall he also reap."

If we consider the overall picture, each human being is given an equal chance, but we don't all have the same starting time. We are all born equal to start with, but not at each birth, since we are all on different steps of the stairway, or on the spokes of the wheel of life. We can recognize others who have not climbed very high on the ladder, and we know when some have made it almost to the top. We tend to associate with those on our own level, because communication with them is easier — on similar wave-lengths.

The "young soul" is prone to be swayed by outside influences and trends of the times; some are blown about like reeds in the wind. More experienced souls, generally referred to as "old souls" will more and more stand up for their principles, and as we grow — like trees buffetted by the storms of life — harder tasks will be given to us. Gradually we shall learn to subsist on very sparse soil, as we are being transferred beyond the timber line on the Himalaya of the mind.

TO A NEW SOUL

Are you a star that fell from heaven,
An angel, just descended to this earth?
Regarding the first time, in innocence,
With wide-eyed wonderment, this world?

Your eyes are bright and fresh,
Even your hair is smiling,
Just as we are when we behold
The wonder of a new-born day.

You are so fresh and full of sunlight,
Your karma still seems light to you.
God-speed, and may you learn it quickly,
You wide-eyed wonder of a new-born soul.

P.S. As Manly P. Hall says: "May this be the end of seeking, and the beginning of becoming."

BUFFETED

We seem like the rolling balls
Injected again and again
Into the Pin Ball machine,
Tough enough to be launched
And re-launched again
Into another life's game -
Can we plan and design,
Figure out orbits,
To anticipate
Pushes and pulls
Attractions, rejections?
We know that we shall
And must pass again,
Between Charybdis and Scylla,
And have to listen again and again
To the sweet song of sirens
That comes over the air
And deflects our attention
From the dangers of life.
The bells may not ring
Ere we hit the last rock
On the road to the next
Intermediate judgment,
The Supreme Court
Of Eternal Justice.
Watch for the knocks
And study the odds -
You cannot escape,
But learning pays off!

TUMBLING

As the cogwheels turn
The tumbler of life,
We are tossed and tumbled,
Stood up and stood down,

Thrown against each other
To polish us nice
Till the grinders smoothen
Our facets, our face.

Only rough diamonds
Will scratch and scrape
The other tough gems
Into smoother shape.

Having finally turned
Every other cheek
To be pummelled and punched,
Till our faces are sleek:

Our facets will shine,
Our diamond will glow
And smoothly slide
To Nirvana row.

P.S. Out from the polishing, rebirthing channel of the pinball machine of life on earth.

WHENCE AND WHITHER

Whence do we come,
And whither do we go?
We'd better make our plans
While there is time to choose.
We cannot die,
So we had better
Watch what we do!
For every guilt
Has to be paid for
Right here on Earth.
Make no mistake,
God's mills grind slowly,
But exceeding fine.
And if the "Lord
Of this world" here
Now does not catch you,
He most surely will,
Next time around!

NOW is the time
To build your house,
For your next life.
You have the choice
Of many mansions,
But YOU make the selection:
YOU submit plan and design
To the chief Architect Divine!

                    C.T.E.

I AM A FLAME

— A flame
Burning in water,
Divine sparks flowing
In constant stream.

— A votive light
In the Cathedral,
Shedding a warm,
Red-golden glow
Into the innermost
Dark recesses
Of the shrine,
And the soul.

* * *

Spreading the light
Is my mission on Earth.

* * *

I am a flame
Burning between two waters
A cosmic spark
In an ocean of flesh.

                    C.T.E.

CARL T. ENDEMANN

ABOUT THE AUTHOR

After an exciting life as a mulinational insurance executive in different countries, Carl T. Endemann settled down in California and has become the author of 5 books, with 3 more in preparation. He has also edited and published several books for others.

Poetry was his first love, but while living in Paris and San Francisco he studied painting under well known French, Spanish and American impressionists. This styule still is his favorite in his paintings, which made several museum shows and are now on exhibit in several galleries. His poems have often been likened to French impressionist paintings.

His travels abroad and friendships with many people of different ethnic backgrounds have opened his mind to the ways and thoughts of people other than the WASP group to which he belongs.

He has lived with Armenian, Chinese, Dutch, English, French, German, Greek, Hawaiian, South American and Swedish people. This deepened his interest in Geography and History, and gradually led to the study of the subjects you will find expounded in this volume.

Carl now lives with his wife, Ranie Maya, in the upper Napa Valley of California, ALTA NAPA, surrounded and inspired by vineyards, as were his ancestors a thousand years ago by the River Rhine.

What are his ideals and ambitions? To be like an "UOMO UNIVERSALE" of the Renaissance, and to study Far Eastern languages.

REBORN IN NAPA VALLEY

I lived for many years in exciting cities like Hamburg, New York, Paris, and San Francisco, with their enchanting waterfronts and cosmopolitan restaurants, and in just as enchanting small towns like Swinemünde and Sausalito. I loved them all. All of them have changed with the passing of the years, as though a doom of decline hung over them. It was not in the cities I was to find my place in the sun.

Astro*Carto*Graphy had indicated that central California was right for me, and it seemed so, but it was only when driving through the vast expanses of vineyards along the Silverado Trail in Napa Valley that I felt I had taken the right fork in the road of life.

The vines were billowing in the wind like the waves of a green sea, like the rollers off the Baltic island of my youth. The vines exhaled fresh oxygen that gave me new inspiration when I watched the eternally self-renewing vines returning to a new life, a new incarnation every spring, as my ancestors had a thousand years ago on the River Rhine.

With every spring I received new inspiration to "come to life" and as the "pruned" vines put forth new growth, new life, so I was inspired to put forth new growth, new endeavors. My harvest this time was poems and I yearned to express something of the beauty of life, and life beyond life. Thus my book on reincarnation, "Voyage Into The Past" came into being.

What better demonstration of eternal life can we find than the annual passing through transition of the vines, which burst into new glory every springtime?

CARL T. ENDEMANN

Bibliography

Blavatsky, Helen P.
THE SECRET DOCTRINE 1888
Theosophical Publishing Company, Ltd., Madras, India

Churchward, Colonel James
THE CHILDREN OF MU 1931
Ives Washburn, Publisher, New York, N.Y.

Ducasse, C.J.
THE BELIEF IN A LIFE AFTER DEATH 1961
Charles G. Thomas, Publisher, Springfield, Ill.

Ehrlich, Max
THE REINCARNATION OF PETER PROUD 1974
Bobbs-Merrill Company, Inc., Indianapolis, Ind.

Emerson, Ralph Waldo
ESSAY ON COMPENSATION IN SELECTED PROSE & POETRY 1950
Rinehart & Company, Inc., New York, N.Y.

Fagan, Cyril
ASTROLOGICAL ORIGINS 1971
Llewellyn Publications, St. Paul, Mn.

Gauquelin, Michel
THE COSMIC CLOCKS 1967
Avon Books, New York, N.Y.
COSMIC INFLUENCES ON HUMAN BEHAVIOR 1973
ASI Publishers, Inc., New York, N.Y.
THE SCIENTIFIC BASIS OF ASTROLOGY 1966
Stein & Day, Publishers, New York, N.Y.

Georg, Eugen
THE ADVENTURE OF MANKIND 1931
E.P. Dutton, New York, N.Y.

Graham, David
THE PRACTICAL SIDE OF REINCARNATION 1976
Prentice-Hall, Inc., Englewood Cliffs, N.J.

Guirdham, Arthur
THE CATHARS AND REINCARNATION 1970
Theosophical Publishing House, Wheaton, Ill.

Hall, Manly P.
REINCARNATION 1939
THE SECRET DESTINY OF AMERICA 1944
Philosophical Research Society, Los Angeles, Ca.

Head, Joseph and Cranston, S.L.
REINCARNATION: THE PHOENIX FIRE MYSTERY 1977
Crown Publishers, Inc., New York, N.Y.

Heindel, Max
THE ROSICRUCIAN COSMO—CONCEPTION 1940
The Rosicrucian Fellowship Publishers, Ocenside, Ca.

Hodson, Geoffrey
REINCARNATION — FACT OR FALLACY?
THROUGH THE GATEWAY OF DEATH
THE SCHOOL OF WISDOM LECTURE NOTES
Theosophical Publishing House, Wheaton, Ill.

Holroyd, Stuart
PSYCHIC VOYAGES
The Danbury Press

Holzer, Hans
  BORN AGAIN 1970
  Double Day and Company, Garden City, N.Y.

Hoyle, Fred
  FRONTIERS OF ASTRONOMY 1957
  Harper and Row, Publishers, New York, N.Y.

Huett, Lenora and Richardson, Jenny and Wally
  THE PATH TO ILLUMINATION 1973
  Angel Press, Monterey, Ca.

Jensen, Johannes V.
  THE LONG JOURNEY 1923
  Alfred A. Knopf, New York, N.Y.

Kuhn, Alvin Boyd
  SHADOW OF THE THIRD CENTURY 1949
  Theosophical Publishing House, Wheaton, Ill.

Lewis, H. Spencer
  THE MYSTICAL LIFE OF JESUS 1929
  MANSIONS OF THE SOUL 1930
  SELF MASTERY AND FATE WITH THE CYCLES OF LIFE 1929
  The Rosicrucian Press, Ltd., San Jose, Ca.

"Magnus Incognito"
  THE SECRET DOCTRINE OF THE ROSICRUCIANS 1918
  Advanced Thought Publishing Co., Chicago, Ill.

Moody, Raymond A. Jr., M.D.
  LIFE AFTER LIFE 1975
  Bantam Books, Inc., New York, N.Y.

Moore, Marcia and Douglas, Mark
  REINCARNATION, KEY TO IMMORTALITY 1968
  Arcane Publications, York Harbor, Maine

Nouy, Le Comte de
  HUMAN DESTINY 1947
  Longmans, Green and Co., New York, N.Y.

Plato
  THE REPUBLIC OF PLATO
  Oxford University Press

Playfair, Guy Lyon
  THE INDENFINITE BOUNDARY 1976
  St. Martin's Press, New York, N.Y.

Playfair and Hill
  THE CYCLES OF HEAVEN 1978
  St. Martin's Press, New York, N.Y.

Stearn, Jess
  THE SEARCH FOR A SOUL 1973
  Doubleday and Company, Garden City, N.Y.

Steiner, Rudolf
  COSMIC MEMORY
  Rudolf Steiner Publishing, Blauvelt, N.Y.

Stevens, Henry Bailey
  THE RECOVERY OF CULTURE 1949
  Harper and Brothers, Publishers, New York, N.Y.

Swedenborg, Emmanuel
  COMPENDIUM of THE THEOLOGICAL AND SPIRITUAL WRITINGS of EMMANUEL
  SWEDENBORG 1853
  Crosby and Nichols, Boston, Mass.

Szekely, Edmund Bordeaux
    THE GREATNESS IN THE SMALLNESS 1978
    International Biogenic Society, Cartago, Costa Rica

Van Deusen, Edmund
    ASTRO—GENETICS 1976
    Doubleday and Company, Garden City, N.Y.

Viereck and Eldridge
    MY FIRST TWO THOUSAND YEARS 1929
    Duckworth, 3 Henrietta Street,London, England

Wambach, Helen, PhD
    RELIVING PAST LIVES 1978
    Harper and Row, Publishers, New York, N.Y.

ENCYCLOPEDIA of SOURCE ILLUSTRATIONS
    Editor, John Georg Heck
    Morgan and Morgan Publishers
    Hastings on Hudson, N.Y. 10706